Praise for *Expand Social Security Now!*

"Read this book before you vote. Few issues are more important to your personal economic future. Steven Hill shows what's at stake, and he offers solutions that Americans of all stripes can agree on."
—ROBERT B. REICH,
AUTHOR OF *Saving Capitalism:
For the Many, Not the Few*

"Steven Hill has written a barn burner of a book. Or perhaps I should say 'myth buster,' because he systematically demolishes the false justifications for slashing Social Security. In place of misplaced animus and misleading arguments, he offers a strong case for dramatically expanding America's most successful domestic program in an age of rising inequality and widespread financial insecurity."
—JACOB S. HACKER,
COAUTHOR OF *American Amnesia:
How the War on Government Led Us to Forget
What Made America Prosper*

"Steven Hill has written a vigorous defense of Social Security, the country's most important social program. While most political debate in recent years has focused on ways to cut Social Security or privatize it, Hill goes in the opposite direction and argues for a robust expansion. Hill proposes a Social Security program that would be adequate by itself to support a middle-class retirement."
—DEAN BAKER,
COFOUNDER OF THE CENTER FOR ECONOMIC AND
POLICY RESEARCH, AND AUTHOR OF *Getting Back to Full
Employment: A Better Bargain for Working People*

"*Expand Social Security Now!* is a must-read. It is about the soul of our nation and what kind of society we want to be. Steven Hill lays it out plainly and powerfully, and shows what we can do about it."
—KATRINA VANDEN HEUVEL,
AUTHOR OF *Meltdown: How Greed and
Corruption Shattered Our Financial System
and How We Can Recover*

"*Expand Social Security Now!* is engaging, thought-provoking, and compelling. Hill's bold plan to double Social Security benefits is a brilliant response to our looming retirement-income crisis, and to the nation's rising income inequality. The book is a must-read for all those who hope to enjoy an independent and dignified retirement."
—NANCY J. ALTMAN,
COAUTHOR OF *Social Security Works!*

"Steven Hill has produced a dynamite handbook for angry Americans who seek to take back democracy. The true contest is not Republicans versus Democrats. It is the American people versus Washington. And this is the sleeper issue the people can win. The governing elites in both parties are trying to eviscerate Social Security—arguably the most successful and most popular program created by the federal government. Hill explains why the political insiders and their Wall Street patrons are wrong about Social Security. He shows us how to mobilize to defeat the power elites and expand Social Security rather than destroy it."
—WILLIAM GREIDER,
AUTHOR OF *Come Home, America: The Rise and Fall (and Redeeming Promise) of Our Country*

"The ability of a people to retire with dignity is the hallmark of a great nation, and with the inadequate 401(k)s of the Inequality Era, our nation is falling short. Steven Hill's proposal to expand a twentieth-century idea for a twenty-first-century labor market is at once commonsense and radical."
—HEATHER C. McGHEE,
PRESIDENT OF DEMOS

"This book is terrific! Steven Hill proposes specific ways to expand Social Security and make it fairer for everyone. He also busts the myth that Social Security is 'broke' and shows why it matters more than ever in this election year—especially for anyone who wants to be elected to public office, or even the presidency."
—STEPHANIE TAYLOR,
COFOUNDER OF THE PROGRESSIVE CHANGE CAMPAIGN COMMITTEE

EXPAND SOCIAL SECURITY NOW!

Books by Steven Hill

Raw Deal:
How the "Uber Economy" and Runaway Capitalism
Are Screwing American Workers

10 Steps to Repair American Democracy:
2012 Elections Edition

Europe's Promise:
Why the European Way Is the Best Hope
in an Insecure Age

Fixing Elections:
The Failure of America's Winner Take All Politics

Whose Vote Counts? (with Robert Richie)

EXPAND SOCIAL SECURITY NOW!

*How to Ensure Americans
Get the Retirement They Deserve*

STEVEN HILL

BEACON PRESS
BOSTON

Beacon Press
Boston, Massachusetts
www.beacon.org

Beacon Press books
are published under the auspices of
the Unitarian Universalist Association of Congregations.

19 18 17 16   8 7 6 5 4 3 2 1

This book is printed on acid-free paper that meets the uncoated paper
ANSI/NISO specifications for permanence as revised in 1992.

Text design by Wilsted & Taylor Publishing Services

LIBRARY OF CONGRESS CATALOGING-IN-PUBLICATION DATA

Names: Hill, Steven, author.
Title: Expand social security now! : how to ensure
Americans get the retirement they deserve / Steven Hill.
Description: Boston : Beacon Press, [2016] | Includes
bibliographical references and index.
Identifiers: LCCN 2015040023 | ISBN 978-0-8070-2843-8 (pbk. :
alk. paper) | ISBN 978-0-8070-2844-5 (ebook)
Subjects: LCSH: Social security—United States. | Retirement
income—United States. | Fiscal policy—United States. |
Finance, Public—United States. | United States—Social
policy. | United States—Politics and government—2009– .
Classification: LCC HD7125.H536 2016 | DDC 368.4/300973—
dc23 LC record available at http://lccn.loc.gov/2015040023

To President Franklin D. Roosevelt
and that amazing generation of New Deal leaders
who understood that since we all share the same risks,
we might as well collectively insure ourselves against them.
And thus was born . . . Social Security.

Contents

EXPAND SOCIAL SECURITY NOW!

High Stakes
for the American People

*"The test of our progress is not whether we add
more to the abundance of those who have much;
it is whether we provide enough for those who
have too little."*

—PRESIDENT FRANKLIN DELANO ROOSEVELT [1]

*"We are in the midst of a real and growing
retirement crisis—a crisis that is shaking the
foundations of what was once a vibrant and
secure middle class."*

—US SENATOR ELIZABETH WARREN [2]

For more and more Americans, the dream of a secure retirement
has become increasingly threatened. The hope for an old age
spent in simple comfort and well-being, surrounded by family
and community, is sadly fading for many. This transition—which
we are told is as inevitable and natural as the laws of gravity—is
part of the ongoing crumbling of the New Deal safety net and
social contract that has protected American workers, families,
and communities for decades. And this is not happening because
America is broke and sagging under the weight of too much debt,
as some have claimed. No, this threat to the nation's future is

self-inflicted—it's because we have the wrong policies, and just as crucially, the wrong politics.

The correct policies would be eminently affordable—if the politicians in Washington, DC, could cease their fealty to wealthy special interests, as well as their partisan sandbox play, and act in the national interest. Instead, both Democrats and Republicans have waged a monstrous two-headed game of brinkmanship that only makes sense to those locked inside the hall of mirrors of our nation's capital.

According to today's mistaken Beltway consensus, the United States cannot afford to pay for the present level of Social Security benefits for retirees in future generations, and so benefits must be cut. This consensus is not only wrong in its diagnosis but also mistaken in its prescriptions—and potentially disastrous in its consequences.[3]

The attack on Social Security—the hugely popular program formally known as Old Age and Survivors Insurance (OASI)—is one of the best examples of a larger battle royal that should be headlined: "We the People versus Washington." We are locked in a historic struggle over whether our nation is truly "of, by, and for the people," or if, instead, it is ruled by an insider ring of powerful economic and political elites who are extracting the best of our nation for themselves.

In the battle over Social Security and other safety-net components, in a very real sense US democracy itself is at stake. Over the next few years, we are going to discover whether the American republic, which has been the model for so much good in the world, is fated to fulfill the prophecy of late nineteenth-century Italian political scientist Gaetano Mosca and his "ruling class" theory, which said that, at the end of the day, "the history of all societies has been, is, and will be, the history of dominant minorities."[4]

To understand how far the Beltway consensus has drifted away from popular opinion, consider these words of a national leader from a previous era:

> Should any political party attempt to abolish Social Security, un-
> employment insurance and eliminate labor laws and farm pro-

grams, you would not hear of that party again in our political history. There is a tiny splinter group, of course, that believes you can do these things. Among them are . . . a few Texas oil millionaires and an occasional politician or business man from other areas. Their number is negligible, and they are stupid.

Yes, "stupid" is what the man said. Those blunt words, not very diplomatic, were penned by President Dwight Eisenhower—a Republican and military hero—in a letter to his brother Edgar in 1954. But flash forward sixty years, and even though the program that provides "old-age and survivors insurance" is extremely popular—even a supermajority of Republicans favor it—and even though three-quarters of Americans heavily depend on Social Security in their elderly years, the revered program has become a political football.

Many conservatives and special interest groups have called for austerity-like "entitlement reform," and even leading Democrats, including President Barack Obama and Hillary Clinton, and before them President Bill Clinton, have knelt at the altar of proposing cuts "to save Social Security." Yet as this book will show, not only are cuts to Social Security not necessary financially; in fact, the United States should be *expanding* Social Security—so that it provides a more secure and portable retirement for America's well-deserving retirees, and acts as an "automatic stabilizer" for the new high-tech economy that is rapidly powering to the forefront of the twenty-first century.

Perhaps the most puzzling aspect of the bipartisan undermining of Social Security is that the program itself remains wildly popular across the political spectrum. A survey from the National Academy of Social Insurance (NASI) found overwhelming backing among voters in both major parties, with 69 percent of Republicans and 84 percent of Democrats agreeing "it is critical to preserve Social Security benefits for future generations, even if it means increasing the Social Security taxes."[5] You read that correctly—almost 70 percent of Republicans back a tax *increase*. And that's not all. More than seven in ten Republicans and nine in ten Democrats agree that those in the top income brackets should pay more Social Security tax (specifically that they should be taxed on all of their earnings, not just wages under $118,500, which is the upper limit for Social Security's payroll tax as of 2015). Three-fourths of respondents opposed increasing the retirement age to seventy or reducing the cost-of-living increases. Majorities opposed any measures to balance Social Security's future finances by reducing benefits.

And unlike the Beltway politicians, average voters are capable of making nuanced trade-offs and compromises to address the challenges faced by America's ailing retirement system. In NASI's survey, fully 68 percent of Republicans, 74 percent of Democrats, and 73 percent of independents favored a package of reforms that included gradually eliminating the payroll cap so that wealthy earners—millionaires and billionaires—have to pay their fair share of the Social Security tax on their full income; gradually increasing the tax paid by all workers by 1 percent over twenty years; increasing the cost-of-living adjustments; and raising Social Security's minimum benefit level to ensure retirees stay out of poverty.[6] That package would turn Social Security's projected financing gap, predicted to occur sometime in the 2030s, into a small surplus.[7] And notice: every partisan viewpoint had to give something for this package of reforms to work. But you know what? Regular people, guided by common sense, were able to figure it out. So could Congress, if its members really listened to their constituents. Problem solved, simple as that.

And yet nothing is simple when it comes to the politicians' bipartisan bumbling of America's retirement crisis. Here's a clue why: research reveals one group of Americans that does not like, and in fact is opposed to, Social Security—the very wealthy. A recent study measuring policy preferences between the wealthy and the general public showed differences of opinion on a range of issues. One of the biggest gaps is over Social Security—by a wide margin most Americans at the top 1 percent income bracket want it cut.[8] That's where the bipartisan consensus apparently gets its marching orders, because the plutocrats have more influence with both Republicans and Democrats than "We the People."

Expand Social Security Now! will show how political and economic elites in both the Democratic and Republican parties are selling out everyday Americans and stirring up an artificial and completely unnecessary national retirement crisis. They want us to think that the $2.8 *trillion* surplus in the Social Security Trust Fund is part of a massive government handout, even some kind of socialist experiment that is doomed to collapse, when nothing could be further from the truth. Just like a company pension or life insurance plan, that enormous surplus comes chiefly from premiums—in the form of payroll contributions—paid by all US workers. It *belongs* to the workers. It belongs to *us*, it is *our* money; it is an *earned* benefit, not a handout. The government is merely holding it for us, for all Americans, until it is needed in our elderly years.

Social Security in many ways is the "canary in the mineshaft," the heart of the prosperous post–World War II society that launched an affluent middle class that has been the envy of the world. Rather than cut Social Security, I will demonstrate (as others have before) that it's possible to expand it and secure a brighter future not only for the nation's retirees but for younger generations as well. *There is no inter-generational war over Social Security*, though some of the "experts" have unconscionably tried to foment one.

This book will argue that, rather than cutting Social Security, we should make its *expansion* the core remedy for stabilizing the US retirement system and the broader national economy. More specifically, we should *double* Social Security's individual monthly payout for the 43 million Americans who receive individual retirement benefits and create a new system that I call Social Security Plus. According to the Social Security Administration, it currently costs about $662 billion annually to provide benefits to those retirees, so doubling that amount sounds expensive and unaffordable.[9] But this book will outline various ways to pay for it. It's not as difficult as it sounds. Some relatively simple and straightforward changes to how retirement is funded can take us a long way toward making the US system better adapted to the realities of today's new, high-tech driven economy. And we can accomplish this without spending a dime more in government money or national wealth than what is already being spent on the nation's retirement system.

The challenge before us really boils down to one key concept: tax fairness. In reality, the current tax system is unfair in a lot of ways. And one of those ways is how Social Security is funded. For example, we have a progressive income tax system, which means that higher-earning Americans pay not only more income tax but a *higher percentage* of their income in income tax. That system is based on a long-held principle that those who are better off, and who have benefited the most from society's rich garden that we all have had a hand in tilling, should give back to the garden and help maintain it. In many ways that "gardener's principle" is one of the foundations of civilization itself.

Yet as we will see, when it comes to Social Security, we actually have a *regressive* tax system. Those who earn more income actually pay a *lower percentage* of their income into the Social Security Trust Fund. That's because according to the current rules any income above $118,500 is not taxed for Social Security purposes. And any income obtained through dividends and capital gains—which is how many affluent people with a lot of investments make most of their wealth—is completely untaxed for Social Security purposes. Consequently, a chauffeur pays a 6.2 percent Social Security payroll tax on her salary, while the corporate executive she drives around pays less than 2 percent of his salary. A multimillionaire banker pays an even lower percentage, less than 1 percent. In this upside-down world, a billionaire pays the same amount of money into Social Security as someone who makes $118,500 a year. No other government program is funded through such a regressive tax. Medicare, defense, environmental programs, education, and more are all, for the most part, funded by a progressive tax system in which those who have greater means contribute more.

In addition, our tax code includes a vast number of federal deductions, exclusions, deferrals, and subsidies that vastly favor wealthier Americans. Indeed, the tax code is riddled with labyrinths, loopholes, and hidden trapdoors that only tax attorneys and accountants can figure out. It is like a maze in a video game, where you enter room after room, and if you have the right specialized knowledge and experience you can run through the maze and pick up the video game equivalent of gold coins and treasure chests. Since only better-off people can afford tax attorneys and accountants, or even earn sufficient income to benefit from these deductions, most of these tricks of the tax code conceal their benefits from the vast majority of Americans. As we will see, these tricks and loopholes have odd-sounding names, so technical in nature that they seem innocuous and obscure—"capital gains," and its twisted offspring "step-up in basis" and "carried interest."

But they are not innocuous, even as they have been hiding in plain sight. They amount to real money being steered into the pockets of wealthier Americans who have access to the experts who know how to run through the maze and pick up the gold coins. If these tax loopholes are eliminated, we would free up tens of billions—not millions, but *billions*—of dollars that can be targeted at better uses, such as funding Social Security Plus.

At the same time, we should redesign other components of the US retirement system, including 401(k)s, IRAs, private pensions, and even homeownership's impact on retirement, so that they better fit with the type of society we are becoming. After a quarter century of experimentation with using the tax code to encourage private savings via various incentives, we now know that the vast majority of these benefits also go to the upper 10–20 percent of income earners. For the rest of Americans, this system has utterly failed to help them save for a secure retirement (which should hardly be surprising—with average Americans' wages remaining flat for over two decades, it's hard to save when you don't have sufficient income). The proposal for Social Security Plus is based upon the commonsense notion that we should build upon what works rather than what has failed. Instead of compounding failure by expanding the flawed system of tax-favored private savings accounts—that is, 401(k)s, IRAs, and other personal deductions—we should drastically reduce their importance and even think about eliminating them altogether. This also applies to private employer-based pensions (which are quickly disappearing anyway), since doing so would provide some of the revenue needed for dramatically expanding the popular and successful Social Security program.

By shifting federal government tax and expenditure priorities that right now benefit a small number of better-off people, and focusing them instead on the vast majority of Americans, we can enact a retirement system that will work for all of us instead of some of us.

That's why, when it comes to the nation's retirement system, the solution to our current predicament boils down to a simple formula:

TAX FAIRNESS = RETIREMENT SECURITY

And a secure retirement for all Americans is linked to other extremely important national goals, such as a prosperous and robust economy, one that has automatic stabilizers built in that help to right the ship during economic downturns.

So our simple formula becomes:

TAX FAIRNESS = RETIREMENT SECURITY = ECONOMIC STABILITY

However, this is not a call for some "big government" intervention, but rather for a "smart government" solution, using government's unique power to regulate and to bring various stakeholders to the table.* It is driven by a pragmatic recognition that, given all of the other options that have been proposed, this expansion of Social Security is the one that will actually maintain some semblance of the middle-class society that has helped make the United States the envy of the world. Call it the best solution, or call it the least-worst solution, if you wish. To get ready. for the new high-tech economy that is barreling down the turnpike like a steamroller at Indy 500 speeds, a significant chunk of

---

* To be clear, besides being a core part of the nation's retirement system, the overall Social Security program also includes disability and survivor benefits, which help Americans and their loved ones in the event they become disabled, or in case a breadwinner of a family dies prematurely. Social Security is a powerfully comprehensive insurance program in that way, and the disability and survivor benefits are fundamental components of what makes ours a civilized society. But in this book I will only discuss the retirement portion of the Social Security program.

"workplace-based" safety-net supports for American workers—not only retirement but also health-care, unemployment, and injured-worker compensation; paid sick days; vacation; and other features—must become individually based instead of workplace-based. The safety net must become attached to individual workers and follow them around, no matter their work situation, who their employer is, or even if they are unemployed. Supports for workers must become what are known as fully "portable."

I will show why designing a more portable and robust retirement system needs to be part of the new economy that is emerging, in which more and more workers are losing the "good" jobs of the New Deal society and becoming insecure freelancers, independent contractors, temps, and part-time workers in a "freelance society." As time goes on, more workers will no longer have a single employer and a regular full-time job, but instead will cobble together their income from multiple employers, each offering part-time contingent work and none legally responsible for providing a safety net to their freelancing workers. An Oxford University study of over seven hundred occupations found that a significant chunk of existing US jobs are at risk of elimination from computerization over the next twenty years[10]—tens of millions of jobs threatened by "technological unemployment," as economist John Maynard Keynes once called it.[11] Other experts dispute the extent of computerization's impact, but all agree that the US economy is about to go through a major technological shift. We have no choice but to position Social Security to play a much more robust role in the evolution of this new economy.

Defending a Sacred Trust

The US retirement system, with all its components parts, has been the yellow brick road leading to a pot of gold at the end of most workers' careers. It has demonstrated its value decade after decade, and it has been one of the most successful government programs of all time. And yet it is threatened now more than ever by leading politicians, business leaders, and media pundits who insist, despite all the facts to the contrary, that Social Security benefits are no longer affordable and must be cut. To the extent that there is another "side" of this debate over whether to cut Social Security, it comes mainly from those who are on the defensive, fighting merely to maintain Social Security as it is, or those who propose incremental reforms to preserve the status quo—even though the status quo is increasingly inadequate. Neither "side" of this debate is addressing the reality of America's retirement crisis.

As we will see, although two of the three legs of the "retirement stool" have been sawed back to nubs, the only bipartisan proposal currently under consideration calls for cuts to the last remaining leg—Social Security. Each partisan side of the aisle has its own preferred way of doing that, but don't be fooled: they amount to the same thing. They will make cuts in the ever-popular program that has long been one of the glues of our society, a sacred trust between generations and a testament to American family values. Even President Barack Obama at times has proposed his own type of cuts. Both sides are presenting the same basic face, which is biased toward the affluent and skewed toward private savings, rather than doubling down on the type of "wage insurance" that has been so successful—Social Security.

Naturally, the entitlement busters don't always announce their scheming plans. Instead, they have been waging a stealth campaign, and so far, it's working. They have plans to cut Social Security benefits, privatize our contributions, increase the retirement age, minimize the cost-of-living increase, and turn the whole thing over to Wall Street managers who will reap a fortune in charging fees and premiums to oversee this transformation. We saw how well that worked out with the hedge fund–stoked home mortgage crisis that collapsed the global economy in 2008. Not enough people sounded the alarm on that one until it was too late. This time, we have to expose the banksters and make the politicians listen. We need a "people's plan" for fixing the retirement mess that the bipartisan consensus has dropped into our laps.

Imagine if the front page of every newspaper, or if the lead story on every media news show, blared a headline that shouted "Washington and Wall Street Conspiring to Gut America's

Retirement—and Only 'We, the People,' Can Stop Them.'" Would Americans stand on the sidelines and let that happen? Would they tune out with their favorite TV shows and Twitter celebrities? Or like Paul Revere and the Minutemen, would they answer the call? I believe Americans would respond with pitchforks and torchlight parades, marching to dump the tea into the harbor.

But most Americans don't realize what is happening, or what is at stake. The current crisis provides a crucial opportunity to rethink the system as a whole, and to redesign this "third rail" of politics for the challenges of the twenty-first century. In this book, I will show not only how to expand Social Security but also how to pay for it, and why that would be good for America's retirees, good for America's businesses, and good for our nation's continued standing in the world as a beacon of hope and prosperity. My proposed plan for Social Security Plus—including a doubling of the individual payout—would form the core of a new kind of deal for American workers. There hasn't been a serious call for Social Security expansion in a couple of decades, yet recently more political leaders and media pundits have raised this possibility. In a relatively short period of time, Social Security expansion is being discussed by more and more people as a serious solution to America's retirement crisis. The political needle has moved, and a moment may be arriving that will reset this landscape.

This book provides a blueprint for how to move forward. Simply by making our retirement system *more fair*, we will vastly improve everyday Americans' lives, including the younger generations, and preserve the power of hope in our nation's dream. By making it *more innovative*, we will design a retirement system that has the ability to preserve Main Street's crucial place in the emerging high-tech, new economy. And by making it *more stable*, we will put the national economy on a more solid footing, preserving the robust middle-class society that made the United States a great magnet for the world.

More fair, more innovative, and more stable . . . and better adapted to the realities of today's new economy. Social Security Plus will contribute to a solid foundation from which to build a strong and vibrant twenty-first-century economy.

CHAPTER ONE

What's at Stake

Meet Howard and Jean, an older couple I know, who like so many Americans of the "greatest generation" plugged into the New Deal world that promised a secure lunch pail for the middle class. Howard is a World War II veteran who became a mechanic; when he was younger he worked on automobiles for a local Chevy dealership, and then on commercial airliners for United Airlines out at the airport. Jean was a housewife and part-time sales clerk. They worked hard, saved their earnings, bought a house, opened passbook bank accounts for their five kids to save their dimes, sent all five of those kids to college. As the years stretched on, they began to prepare for their retirement. But something bad happened along the way to their retirement plans.

A university education is expensive (especially in the United States), and other rising living expenses began to nibble away at Jean and Howard's middle-class lifestyle. As with so many of their fellow working-class Americans, their wages didn't rise as fast as prices for a couple of decades, nor as fast as for other Americans enjoying a wealthier life. So at a certain point, Howard and Jean decided to take out a second mortgage on their home. It seemed like a perfectly good idea, lots of people were doing it. Their bank's loan officer actually encouraged them; indeed, the friendly loan officer suggested they add on tens of thousands of dollars more beyond the value of their home just so they would have a bit of a cushion for themselves. Interest rates were reasonable, and the value of their home had been increasing in recent years. The loan officer showed them the charts—of what the value of their house had been, what it was now, how much it had increased recently, and where it likely would be in . . . five years, ten years. Heck, it almost seemed like free money, this second mortgage.

Indeed, it was free money, their own personal ATM . . . until it wasn't. When the housing market crashed in 2008, so did Howard and Jean's retirement plans. They had sunk most of their savings into their home since, like many Americans, their home was also their piggy bank. Across the nation, the collapse of the housing market in 2008 and the subsequent loss of approximately $8 trillion in housing-based wealth amounted to a direct hit on the nation's retirement security. Like millions of other Americans, the value of Howard and Jean's house plummeted, and while it has recovered some of its value, it is still worth less today than the mortgage they owe on it. They are what is known as "underwater," a graphic but accurate term for their plight, which is shared by nearly 10 million Americans—almost a fifth of all homeowners—who are still financially drowning.[1] Their house, which had been a big part of their retirement future, was now a lead stone around their necks, with the water rising.

Besides owning their own home, Howard and Jean had been thrifty and managed to save a modest amount of money—about $55,000—which they had invested into a 401(k) retirement plan through Howard's workplace. But like the small number of other middle-class Americans fortunate enough to save a bit— three-quarters of workers nearing retirement have less than $30,000 in their 401(k)[2]—they had invested that small nest egg into several mutual funds. Unfortunately, the amount of their savings was nearly cut in half by the stock market collapses of 1999–2000 and 2008–2009. In a matter of a few years, their retirement plans had been shipwrecked as a result of the depreciation in value of both their home and private savings. As they readied for retirement in 2010, their financial prospects had been deluged by a flood of bad news.

Fortunately, Howard and Jean had another unshakeable asset

to depend on—Social Security. They had paid into the Social Security fund all their working lives, not always sure what this 6.2 percent deduction from their paycheck was good for, and they were susceptible to arguments from fiscal conservatives that Social Security should be turned into private retirement accounts so Howard and Jean could keep more of their wages in their pockets. But suddenly, in the depths of their financial flooding, Howard and Jean understood *exactly* why Social Security was important—it created a buffer between them and the whirlpool threatening to suck them down.

While Social Security was their thank-God life jacket, as a life jacket it is rather small. By design, Social Security is only supposed to replace about 30–40 percent of your wages at retirement; yet most financial advisors say you will need 70–80 percent of preretirement earnings to live comfortably.[3] So Howard and Jean really had to tighten their belts, and their middle-class standard of living took a big hit. But at least they did not end up destitute or homeless. Theirs is not a happy story, but the ending of that tale could have been far worse.

Howard and Jean are not the only older Americans in this situation. Many baby boomers, seniors, and soon-to-be's are facing similar circumstances, particularly in the aftermath of the worst economic collapse in the United States since the Great Depression. But what has become known as the Great Recession was just the latest disruption to show that the working life can be a precarious one.

According to the Economic Policy Institute, any Americans who started their working careers in the mid-1960s have witnessed seven recessions—in 1969, 1973, 1980, 1981, 1990, 2001, and 2008—and have lived through inflation, stagflation, oil shocks, oil rationing, the stock market crash of 1987, the savings and loan collapse, the bursting of the dot-com bubble, the bursting of the housing bubble, and the stock market crash of 2008. Add to that the real-estate and leveraged-buyout implosions of the early 1990s; the Enron and WorldCom bankruptcies in the early 2000s; the meltdown of Lehman Brothers; the bailout of AIG, the financial industry, and the auto companies; the issuing of IOUs by the nation's largest state, California, to cover its debts; and a spotty recovery following the worst economic collapse since the Great Depression. In addition, working Americans have seen the national unemployment rate climb above 10 percent twice, and all this during a time that has seen virtually no wage growth for the vast majority and a decline in traditional retirement pensions.[4]

Even in the midst of this Superman-sitting-on-Kryptonite economic recovery, the Chinese bubble collapse in August 2015, which led to a huge stock market sell-off around the world (ig- nominiously named the China Syndrome), showed how fragile the global stock markets remain—how could any sane person possibly suggest the markets as a suitable target for investing your life's savings? The last several decades have been one hellacious roller-coaster ride, with casualties scattered all across the pock- marked landscape in which 145 million working Americans are toiling away. For all but the most well off, navigating the ups and downs of the economy has not been easy.

Since the 1930s, Americans of all political stripes were lucky that they had not only Social Security but also other govern- ment programs to fall back on. Howard and Jean are not the only Americans who, when faced with a tough situation that threat- ened their and their family's economic vitality, reached out and grasped the "visible hand" of government. Hundreds of millions of Americans over the last three-quarters of a century have bene- fited from the New Deal society that was forged decade by decade, law by law, in the aftermath of the Great Depression. President Franklin Roosevelt embraced the unique capacity of government to pull people together and create pools of social insurance that shielded all Americans against the risks and vicissitudes that we all face in common. Besides Social Security, other federal laws and national programs—a long alphabet soup of policies that FDR and successor presidents passed—have shaped the world in which all Americans alive today grew up. These include Medi- care, Medicaid, the Family and Medical Leave Act, student fi- nancial aid, the Federal Housing Administration, the Fair Labor Standards Act, the National Labor Relations Act, the Occupa- tional Safety and Health Act, Equal Employment Opportunity, the Civil Rights Act, laws against discrimination, and laws for the environment and consumer protection.

Our understanding of who we are as a people is inseparable from these policies—yet we don't always recognize it, and many Americans today who are most dependent on these programs like to gleefully bash and deride government. Forty-four percent of Social Security beneficiaries say they have never used a government program; so do 60 percent of recipients of the federal home mortgage interest deduction, 43 percent of unemployment insurance recipients, and 40 percent of Medicare recipients.[5] Each of these programs and laws were passed, with painstaking effort, because they responded to specific situations and conditions in which many Americans—including the most vulnerable, such as the elderly and children—ended up in tough circumstances through no fault of their own, but because of the roller-coaster swings of the economy.

But the New Deal system wasn't created by the wealthy and patrician Roosevelt, and the political and business leaders of the time, merely as an act of charity or compassion for the "one-third of a nation ill-housed, ill-clad, ill-nourished" (as President Roosevelt described our country in his famous Second Inaugural Address).[6] Following the devastation of the Great Depression, it was also a way of remaking the broader macroeconomy into one that was more stable, and of using government's levers of fiscal stimulus, popularized by British economist John Maynard Keynes, to grow the economic pie. That in turn fostered a broadly shared prosperity, which gave rise to the middle class, which became the consumer engine that purchased the goods and services produced by America's businesses. It was a virtuous circle, and while the system wasn't perfect, it worked—it created the highest standard of living for more people in human history. That in turn made the United States the envy of the world, with the middle-class dream becoming an important part of our nation's allure to people everywhere, which gave America more clout on the global stage.

But beginning in the 1970s, the United States engine started losing some of its steam. The plight of the middle class grew more tenuous, resulting in stagnant wages, less job security, the decline of health benefits and the safety net, and the cracking of Americans' nest eggs when their savings and homes deflated after the collapse of the stock and housing bubbles. Over the last three decades, the US economy has more than doubled in size, but most of the benefits from that growth have gone into the pockets of a fortunate few. Corporate profits are at their highest level in at least eighty-five years, while employee compensation is at its lowest level in sixty-five years.[7] The Federal Reserve's Survey of Consumer Finances found that the top 10 percent of families own 75.3 percent of the nation's wealth, while the share of wealth held by the bottom 50 percent of families has fallen to just 1.1 percent.[8] Income inequality is now as bad as it was in 1928,[9] just before the Great Depression, with the top one-tenth of 1 percent of Americans—a mere 160,000 families[10]—now owning nearly a quarter of the nation's wealth, a share that has doubled over the last few decades. Incredibly, the share of wealth held by the bottom 90 percent is no higher today than during our grandparents' time.[11] It's as if the New Deal had never existed.

And future prospects do not look much brighter. Even as corporations have seen a 30 percent rise in profits since the Great Recession in 2008,[12] wages as a share of national income fell to their lowest point since after World War II.[13] Real median household income is now 8 percent lower than it was in 2007.[14] Many of the jobs that were lost during the Great Recession of 2008 were what used to be considered "good jobs"—they offered decent pay, health care, retirement, and a comprehensive safety net, with a measure of job security. Now, nearly a fifth of the job growth since the recession ended has been in temporary jobs,[15] and nearly half of the new jobs created in the so-called "recovery" pay only a bit more than minimum wage. Six years into the recovery, the economy had nearly 2 million fewer jobs in mid- and higher-wage industries than before the recession and 1.85 million more jobs in lower-wage industries.[16] Three-fourths of Americans now live paycheck to paycheck, with little to no emergency savings to rely on if they lose their job.[17] The fears of the middle class, which the Tea Party and politicians like Donald Trump have exploited masterfully, are not paranoia. Their standard of living is in fact eroding.

Yet as bad as the impacts of the Great Recession have been, it did not create the retirement crisis by itself. Rather, the causes are rooted in the larger fundamental economic shifts of the last thirty years. Deregulation, deindustrialization, automation, and hyper-financialization of the economy have all contributed to this mudslide over the cliff. Looking ahead, the shape of the future is coming increasingly into view, and it's clear that other long-term trends warn of additional risks for the middle and working classes.

A 2015 survey from the Freelancers Union and Upwork found that more than one in three Americans—54 million workers—did freelance work in the past year.[18] Other estimates predict that within ten years nearly half of the 145 million employed Americans—60–70 million workers—could well find themselves on shaky grounds, turned into so-called "independent workers," working part time and cobbling together multiple jobs as contractors, temps, gig-preneurs, and contingent workers.[19] Even an increasing number of regularly employed, part-time workers are subjected to conditions like "just-in-time scheduling" in which employers dictate the daily work schedule with no employee input or even advance notice, putting these workers on permanent call (and making it impossible for them to plan their lives, hire babysitters, schedule doctor appointments, and more). Increasingly, all of these different categories of workers have little job security, reduced wages, and a deteriorating safety net—including inadequate retirement resources. So-called "sharing economy" companies like Uber, Airbnb, TaskRabbit, Upwork, and Instacart are allegedly "liberating workers" to become "independent" and "their own CEOs," but in reality workers are being forced to take ever-smaller jobs ("gigs," "micro-gigs," and "nano-gigs") and wages while the companies profit handsomely. Even many full-time, professional jobs and occupations are experiencing this precarious shift.

Indeed, in the gigs of the sharing economy, working for these app- and web-based companies, some contractors, rabbits, task-ers, day laborers, and freelancers have multiple employers *in a single day*. The sharing economy's app- and web-based technolo-gies have made it much easier to hire and fire freelancers and contractors, so why would any employer hire full-time workers anymore? We are at the initial stages of the impacts of these new "job brokerage" technologies and how they will affect the labor force over the next several decades. Set to replace the crumbling New Deal society is the darker world of a "freelance society" in which, in the words of one new economy visionary, "companies want a workforce they can switch on and off as needed"[20]—just like a faucet or a television. Hardly a "sharing" economy, it's more correctly described as a "share the crumbs" economy.

Consequently, for Howard and Jean's children and grandchil-dren, the ground looks even shakier than it does for Howard and Jean. Their future is still infused with that age-old American hope and expectation of a generational inheritance, but economic op-portunity and fairness are fading for the younger generations. The New Deal society is slowly disappearing, melting away like the polar ice caps. And that in turn will be greatly destabilizing to the broader macroeconomy. For at the end of the day, if not enough people have sufficient income in their pockets and bank accounts to buy up all the products and services that US com-panies produce, the economy could reach a dangerous disequi-librium. Seventy percent of the economy is driven by consumer spending, but what happens if consumers' capacity to buy starts shriveling up? We could well face the prospect of an "economic singularity," the tipping point at which our economy implodes from too little consumer demand because the wealth has been captured by a small number of powerful economic players who extract the best of our nation for their own private use. Every-one else will be left to scramble for the scraps via the share-the-crumbs economy.

Considering the nation's future, we can see that the American middle and working classes, as well as the poor, are occupying in-creasingly shaky ground. Only affluent Americans have emerged in better shape than before. But for more and more of their fellow Americans, the dream of a secure and stable life, including their retirement prospects, is becoming increasingly dim.

The Shape of the Retirement Crisis

When our current retirement system was conceived after World War II, during the years when Howard and Jean came of age, the foundation for old-age security was understood as a "three-legged stool." The three legs were (1) private, employer-based retirement, like pensions and (much later) 401(k)s; (2) Social Security; and (3) personal savings centered around homeownership. But as we will see, private-sector pensions now are rare, and the number of public-sector employees (and their pensions) has declined. With the housing market crash in 2008, combined with increasing volatility in the stock market and flat wages for all but the wealthiest people, private savings for most Americans hasn't kept up with the need. In the alluring narrative of the American Dream, home-ownership has been not only a means for providing a secure domicile, but also a core element of household savings and retirement plans. The collapse of the housing market and the subsequent loss of approximately $8 trillion in housing-based wealth amounted to a direct hit on retirement security. Some of that has recovered, but the economic prospects of many Americans have not.

Thus, two of the three legs of a stable retirement have been gravely compromised. For far too many Americans, *Social Security is the only leg left.* Three-fourths of Americans depend heavily on Social Security in their retirement years. Indeed, Social Security has been the most effective antipoverty program ever enacted in the United States. Almost half of elderly Americans today would be poor (incomes below the federal poverty line) without Social Security.[21] The program lifts nearly 15 million elderly Americans out of poverty. For nearly two-thirds of elderly beneficiaries, Social Security provides the majority of their cash income. For more than one-third, it provides more than 90 percent of their income. For one-quarter of elderly beneficiaries, Social Security is the sole source of retirement income. Besides retirement security, Social Security also has contributed significantly to income assistance for orphaned children and disabled workers. To those Americans covered under its safety blanket, Social Security has provided a guaranteed living allowance, month by month, when no other income was available. Where will these people turn if the politicians are successful in cutting back the last stable leg of retirement security?

Reliance on Social Security increases with age, as older people are less likely to work and more likely to have depleted their savings. Among those aged eighty or older, Social Security provides the majority of income for 76 percent of beneficiaries and nearly all of the income for 45 percent of beneficiaries. Social Security is particularly important to women and racial and ethnic minorities, who have historically earned lower wages than their white male counterparts because of discrimination. Social Security provides 90 percent or more of income for 55 percent of elderly Hispanic beneficiaries, 49 percent of blacks, and 42 percent of Asian Americans, but for only 35 percent of elderly white beneficiaries. And women constitute 56 percent of Social Security beneficiaries aged sixty-two and older and 67 percent of beneficiaries aged eighty-five and older, and they receive nearly half of Social Security benefits, despite the fact that women pay only 41 percent of Social Security payroll taxes. Millions of Americans are substantially if not wholly dependent on Social Security to keep the snapping jaws of poverty at bay.[22]

However, it's not just lower-income people or women and minorities who have something at stake here. In fact, it is little recognized that middle-income and upper-income households benefit the *most* from Social Security, in terms of dollars and cents. Since those individuals make more income throughout their lives, they actually receive a higher monthly payout than lower-income people. The average Social Security retirement payout in 2015 was $1,334 per month, or $16,008 per year. So a retired couple each receiving the average amount would get over $32,000 together (if they began taking their benefits at full retirement age, which is sixty-six). On average, a sixty-six-year-old man has about seventeen more years to live, and a woman, about twenty. That means their total take from Social Security would be

nearly $600,000 over the course of their lives (adjusted for infla-
tion). In other words, that couple would need a private nest egg
of $600,000, reaped from their own individual investment and
savings efforts, to match the same amount of income they will
receive from Social Security.[23]

And what about the more affluent? A retired couple who
earned at or above the payroll tax ceiling ($118,500 per year in
2015) their entire lives would each receive the maximum benefit
of around $2,660 per month, or $32,000 each per year—nearly
$64,000 a year together (if they begin taking their benefits at
sixty-six). If that couple lives to the average age, Social Security
would provide them a $1.2 million nest egg (again, adjusted for
inflation) for their retirement. That's a lot of money that this couple would have to replace by rolling the dice, that is, by investing
their savings in the casino of the stock market. Good luck.

American workers deserve a good and secure retirement.
There are many reasons that the working life can be a risky one.
Some workers make low wages throughout their lives and can
never save enough; others never had a pension or 401(k) benefits
through their job, or maybe they were laid off and had to spend
their savings to stay afloat until they found a job. Maybe they
became ill, or a family member became ill, and they had to stop
working; or maybe the company they work for, such as the corporate giants WorldCom or Enron, went belly up; or maybe the
stock market crashed and wiped out half of their 401(k) or the
value of their home, which ended up underwater.

Those sorts of unfortunate circumstances have always plagued
our economic destinies. Amidst all the headline splashes today
about everything from the Kardashians to *Game of Thrones* to
the Super Bowl, it's easy to forget why we have a program like
Social Security in the first place. Prior to its launch in 1935, many
elderly people, as well as orphaned children and disabled workers, lived a life of dire poverty. At the time, older citizens had
the nation's *highest* poverty rate. They were a major part of the
one-third who were ill housed, ill clad, and ill nourished. Now
seniors have the *lowest* poverty rate of any age group.[24] More
than any other government program, Social Security has been a

crucial part of raising up the condition of the lowest, the weakest, and the meekest.

It's also easy to forget that Social Security is an *insurance* program. It's not a government handout; we all pay into it as a way of insuring ourselves against the risks and roller-coaster vagaries of life. With the collapse of two out of the three-legs of the retirement stool, Social Security is the last remaining protection against that risk for millions of Americans. Every worker pays for it, paycheck after paycheck, depositing money into the fund. Indeed, Social Security is *wage* insurance—it keeps wages rolling in when we are too old to work. It is also *universal* insurance—that is, it insures *all of us* against the universal risks *we all face.*

Not only that, but once you retire and start receiving your monthly check, the amount is adjusted each year to keep up with inflation, unlike a savings account or investments in stocks and bonds. Private employers don't adjust wages for inflation, and the federal government has left the minimum wage stuck at the same level since 2009. So this unique cost-of-living feature of Social Security is a godsend to many a retiree. Finally, the government administers it very efficiently; the program costs less than one cent of every dollar to administer. PBS *NewsHour*'s Philip Moeller, a retirement expert, says Social Security's cost structure is so efficient that it "would be impossible for any private company to match" it.[25]

Ideology versus Reality

As this book will demonstrate, our political leadership is failing to adjust the US retirement system either to the recent tide of damaging economic events or to the unfavorable shifts of the past several decades. And the nation's future retirees are wholly unprepared for the challenges of the new, high-tech economy. Part of what's preventing us from making the necessary transition is that Americans have this deep-seated perception of ourselves as self-reliant individualists and a "republic of property owners." Yet all the evidence shows that older Americans are more dependent than ever on *publicly* provided retirement income (primarily Social Security) and health care (Medicare). Americans live inside a schizophrenic disconnect between their view of themselves as Jefferson's sturdy, self-reliant yeoman farmer, and the actual reality that their standard of living depends increasingly on an interconnected web of social supports, with government at the center. It's time to connect the dots so that Americans understand this national reality.

Beyond the sometimes mind-numbing details of specific policy discussions, the debate over the US retirement crisis has become high stakes because it's a tug-of-war over what kind of society we are going to be. A simple example illustrates the baggage of old thinking. Currently any earned income above $118,500 is not subject to the Social Security payroll tax deduction. And income acquired from investments via capital gains and dividends isn't taxed at all for Social Security purposes (and at only half the usual rate for income tax). As a result, a secretary making $35,000 a year pays a 6.2 percent Social Security–dedicated payroll tax (with the employer paying another 6.2 percent, for a total of 12.4 percent)—but a lawyer making $500,000 a year in salary pays less than 1.5 percent. Taxed on the full salary, that lawyer would be paying another $24,000 per year in payroll taxes.

But it gets worse. Millionaire investment bankers pay a paltry 0.73 percent, if you just assume all of their income comes from a salary; but if you include wealth obtained through capital gains and dividends, those bankers and other wealthy people pay a much lower percentage of their actual income—much lower than their secretaries, chauffeurs, and domestic servants. The secretary is paying at least eight times the percentage of the banker for Social Security retirement. If the banker paid his or her full share, it would mean $55,000 more per year in payroll taxes—over eight times the current payment. So not only is Social Security's payroll tax very regressive, but it becomes increasingly regressive as one ascends the income scale, even advantaging the megawealthy over the merely wealthy.

Moreover, with inequality having increased dramatically nationwide, and with the ranks of the wealthy swelling, that means an ever-greater share of the national income sucked up by millionaires and billionaires is not subject to Social Security's payroll tax—and is therefore contributing nothing to the Social Security Trust Fund (which is the account where all the payroll deductions reside). Melissa Favreault, an expert at the nonpartisan Urban Institute, says that three decades ago, 90 percent of the nation's wage earnings were taxed for Social Security purposes; that proportion has now shrunk to 83 percent, making an already regressive tax even more so.[26] That slippage might seem small, but it results in a loss of tens of billions of dollars every year from the Social Security fund. Just in 2014, about $60 billion should have gone into the Trust Fund, but instead it was pocketed by the wealthiest Americans. So when you hear that Social Security is going to run short of money sometime during the 2030s, this is a big part of the reason why. Wealthy people are no longer required to contribute their fair share into the nation's retirement system.[27]

The logic for capping the level of income that is subject to Social Security contributions flows out of the fact that this is an insurance system, not a welfare handout. Social Security in effect is insurance against our loss of wages when we retire (or are disabled), and if wealthy people are not eligible to receive a much higher payout, then, some people believe, they should not have to contribute more. That logic has prevailed for decades, but only for Social Security—when it comes to income, property, or sales taxes, no one asserts that if you pay higher taxes, you should be privileged with a claim for more benefits. With the nation's retirement infrastructure increasingly rickety and unstable like a tottering bridge, it's urgent that we revisit this attitude. Removing the income cap and taxing all income brackets equally—a flat tax, in other words—not only would be fairer but in one bold swoop it also would shore up any long-term financing shortfalls and ensure funding for the Trust Fund beyond the 2040s.

Many conservatives have espoused a flat tax on income, but when it comes to Social Security, suddenly a flat tax is ridiculed as a bad idea. Yet opinion polls have demonstrated that most Americans across the political spectrum think that if they pay Social Security tax on their full salary, others should as well. So removing the payroll cap and making all income levels pay according to the same rules would be the fair and financially wise thing to do, and it would be very popular as well.

And yet the US Congress, even when there has been a Democratic majority, has done little to shift its thinking. Politicians in recent years have had virtually no response to the impending retirement crisis. They have refused to remove the payroll cap and tax all income levels the same, or to take other steps to stop the longer-term deterioration of Social Security's funding. Stuck in the rigid ideology of years past, Beltway politicians are obsessively focused on a "pull ourselves up by our bootstraps" austerity regimen. As part of that attitude, leaders in both political parties have advanced plans for cutting Social Security even further than the cuts that were passed on to future generations by the Greenspan Commission in 1983. In another sign of our nation's split personality, even as Americans like Howard and Jean have come to depend increasingly on Social Security, Medicare, and other pillars of a government-sponsored safety net, the attacks on those "entitlements"—a curse word in US politics—have become increasingly furious and shrill.

Lifting the payroll cap is just one example of how a relatively simple tweak to the system can take us a long way toward solidifying the US retirement system and making it better adapted to the realities of today's economy. Other tweaks that will be discussed in this book will take us further down the right road.

Most Americans realize what is at stake in this battle over Social Security. It's reflected in the worry that most Americans feel over their personal finances, including their retirement future. A poll from March 2015 by the National Institute on Retirement Security (NIRS) found that nearly 75 percent of Americans are "highly anxious" about their retirement outlook, and 73 percent agree that the average worker cannot save enough on their own to guarantee a secure retirement. Nearly half of Americans worry that they will have to sell their homes to be financially secure in retirement, with 81 percent saying it is getting harder to prepare for retirement.[28] A poll in August 2015 commissioned by the senior advocacy group AARP found that nearly two of every three respondents expressed concern that Social Security won't provide enough to get by, especially if they have a major health-care expense that drains them financially. Given all that anxiety, it is hardly surprising that nearly seven in ten people fear that they will not have enough savings to last their whole lifetime.[29]

That's what Americans are feeling—but are the politicians listening? The talented generation of American politicians and business leaders in the 1930s, '40s, and '50s tackled head-on the challenge of forging a new deal for the country in the face of a paralyzing economic crisis and devastating second world war. But the current crew of politicians and business leaders have watched helplessly, or even worse have passed one bad policy after another, as the recent national collapse accelerated decades-long trends that are taking major parts of our economy backward to pre–New Deal conditions. Given the worrisome direction of the national economy, and the safe harbor provided for millions of Americans by Social Security, you'd think our nation's leaders would be trying to figure out how to improve the program, and build up on it. Build upon what works, right?

Wrong. After all, why should members of Congress worry about the nation's retirement plans when the Congressional Research Service reports that, in 2013, over six hundred former members received their own federal government pension that averaged anywhere from $42,048 to $71,664 per year (depending on how long ago they retired). They've got theirs, and it appears they have pulled up the drawbridge.[30]

It's important to understand how our nation arrived at this place of precarious retirement prospects. The next chapter will show how a decades-long drift has led us to the edge of this precipice.

CHAPTER TWO

The Collapse of the Three-Legged Stool

For many decades after World War II, a comfortable middle-class existence was possible for an increasing number of Americans. A generation of returning veterans, most of them men, was able to take advantage of the GI Bill to buy a home cheaply, go to college, start a business, and receive other benefits. Millions of men, as well as their families, prospered. A rising tide floated most boats, as the United States created what was at the time the highest standard of living for more people in the history of the world.

This initiated the building of suburbs and rows upon rows of "little pink houses for you and me." Each house became a family's home, which became a repository for the owners' growing stake in the world, contributing substantial wealth to their eventual retirement. Wages were rising, so beyond being able to afford a home mortgage, more and more Americans also began socking away money into their savings accounts. Those savings accounts eventually turned into certificates of deposits (known affectionately as CDs), money market funds (an early prototype of a mutual fund), and other savings vehicles that became popular in the 1970s.[1]

America's postwar businesses also were flush, raking in more profit than ever before. Feeling charitable, many began rewarding employees with benefits like company pensions and, much later, contributions to 401(k)s. The government also had more tax revenue and started offering generous pensions and health care to public employees. Across the country, Americans as individuals and as families enjoyed their rising status in a superpower nation, becoming more affluent and securing their place in the world. Children had better schools, fathers (though not so much mothers, initially) had better jobs, and college graduates had more opportunity (though obviously there were differences in people's fortunes based on race, gender, and region).

And when you became older and it was your turn to retire, the resources that could be marshaled for your retirement and that of other seniors were unprecedented. You had access to a stable and increasingly robust three-legged stool of a retirement system—your monthly Social Security payments, which by law increased with inflation; your company pension, which, like Social Security's annuity, also provided a guaranteed monthly stipend; and your own private savings, which were mostly invested in the sturdy foundation of your home and could be repurposed (sold or remortgaged) in your final years to pay for your elderly needs. Never had a generation of elders been so well treated; instead of being shooed away as too weak and fallow to work or be productive, a castaway fated to live out your final days in poverty and shame (which had always been the usual lot for most old people), more seniors now lived longer than ever and traveled the world as tourists in leisure and comfort. For many Americans it was truly a Golden Era of Retirement, one of the most momentous accomplishments in human history, all of it founded on this three-legged stool.

Yes, the first several decades after World War II was an Ozzie and Harriet world, unleashed by the supernova of the New Deal. And while the reality was never as contented as the myth (especially for certain demographics of Americans), there was considerable affluence in these communities, and more and more people on the whole shared in this prosperity. The great middle class in the United States had arrived, and quickly became the envy of the world.

But then, something happened to shake the foundation. The three legs of the retirement stool began to grow slowly unsteady. They were shaved back and whittled—not by misfortune or ill luck, but by specific government policy. We are a nation of laws and regulations, and the right ones can do marvelous things, but the wrong ones—well, today the stool is not so stable or secure. We live in a very different world today. What happened?

The First Failing Leg of Retirement Security: Pensions and Employer Retirement Plans

The first leg to go was the one provided by private businesses. The pensions of old worked kind of like Social Security's annuity, in which retired employees received monthly benefit payments. These types of employer-based retirement annuities are known in technical jargon as a "defined-benefit plan," and it was not just a type of savings account but a form of insurance. Once it kicked in upon retirement, it provided a monthly stipend for as long as you were alive, what is known as a "life annuity." Typically both the employer and employee contributed to the plan, based on a formula that calculates the contributions, which are actuarially based on the employee's life expectancy, years of service, final salary, normal retirement age, and other factors. The company funded the pensions, hired someone to run the plans (investing the money from the pension fund into the stock market), and was on the hook if its pension fund investments headed south. In essence, with a defined-benefit plan, the employer bears all the investment risk and commits to its employees' retirement needs in perpetuity.

The company pension system worked marvelously well for many workers, but it wasn't perfect because it wasn't "portable"—workers who had a pension with a particular employer would lose the ability to contribute further to and build that pension if he or she left that job. That made a lot of workers reluctant to change jobs, a situation known as "job-lock." But on the whole, the private company pension was a beneficial complement to the monthly Social Security check. The two of them were a dynamic duo of old-age insurance, kind of like the Batman and Robin of retirement. In 1979, nearly four out of ten private-sector workers were covered by an employer-sponsored pension plan, and about 80 percent of employees in medium- and large-size companies still had such plans in 1985. But in a relatively short period of time that changed dramatically—by the mid-2000s, barely 15 percent of private-sector workers had guaranteed payout pensions, including only 32 percent at medium and large companies.[2]

In the public sector, an even higher percentage of workers was covered by pensions. That percentage is still high today, with approximately 78 percent of state and local government employees, and nearly all federal workers, still participating in government-sponsored pension plans.[3] But both the public and private company pensions began running into problems. They were impacted by a baby-boom bulge in the number of retirees, which was entirely expected. But what was not expected was the erratic nature of the stock market during the two financial crises in 2000 and 2008, which led to unanticipated low returns on the investments that helped fund the pensions. Yet another factor was that some public and private pension plans failed to make adequate contributions into their funds, despite making hefty promises to employees, irresponsibly spending employees' contributions on other priorities. Ultimately many private and public pension funds became plagued by inadequate funding and threats of bankruptcy.

Pensions for public employees at federal, state, and local government levels began entering truly worrisome orbits of underfunding, posing a serious threat to their stability. The Federal Employees Retirement System (FERS), which covers federal government employees, has an "unfunded liability"—in other words, it is in debt—to the tune of more than $600 billion.[4] There is no real risk that the federal government will be unable to pay promised benefits, and the situation has been alleviated somewhat by the fact that the number of public-sector workers has declined dramatically in recent years, accelerating as a result of the Great Recession. There are now a million fewer federal employees than when Ronald Reagan left office, and public-sector employment as a percentage of the population is at a thirty-year low.[5]

But at the state and local levels, things look considerably more grim. The Pew Center reports that all state-run retirement systems combined had a shortfall of nearly $1 trillion in 2013, and a total unfunded liability of over $3.4 trillion. That's the gap between the promised pension benefits that governments owe to their workers and the funding available to meet those obligations. The gap had increased by $54 billion from the previous year.[6] This funding gap affects nearly every state, but some are affected worse than others. Some states like Wisconsin and South Dakota are in fine shape, with 100 percent of their pension obligations funded; but other states are in terrible shape, such as Illinois and Kentucky, with only 39 and 44 percent funded. Only fifteen states had an overall funded ratio of 80 percent or higher, which is the level considered "healthy" enough to cover long-term obligations.

California, being the most populous state, has by far the largest unfunded liability of $610 billion, though to its credit 72 percent of that liability was funded as of 2013. California's two largest public retirement programs, the California Public Employee Retirement System (CalPERS) and the California State Teachers Retirement System (CalSTRS), which cover 65 percent of the 4 million state, county, and local employees who are eligible for public pension benefits, reported $62 billion and $74 billion in unfunded liabilities for 2013.[7] In addition to pension liabilities, states are responsible for hundreds of billions of dollars more in other unfunded benefits, including retiree health, dental, and life insurance.

City governments are also beleaguered by underfunding pensions. The Chicago Teachers' Pension Fund was reported in 2012 to be on the brink of collapse.[8] The *New York Times* reported that from 1999 to 2012, the New York City pension for city employees fell to just 63 percent funded from 136 percent. In 2015, the city set aside more than $8 billion for pensions—11 percent of the budget—which is a twelvefold increase in the city's outlay since 2000, when the payments accounted for less than 2 percent of the budget.[9] Other cities like Los Angeles, Boston, Atlanta, and Pittsburgh have also seen funding for their city pensions enter the red zone.[10]

But it's not just public pensions that have been having problems. Not only have the sheer number of private company pensions declined drastically, but most of the ones that remain are in serious financial trouble. US private pensions were some of the hardest hit in the world by the Great Recession and stock market collapse, at one point falling in value by 37 percent from their peak in 2007. Many of them (though not all) have recovered a bit, but it shows the shakiness and unreliability of private pensions dependent on a roller-coaster stock market for the returns that fund their employees' benefits.[11]

Pension plans at some of the largest US corporations are woefully underfunded. Some of the nation's largest companies, which happen to be led by CEOs who have been prominent in their criticisms of Social Security, have huge deficits in their employee pension funds. These companies include General Electric and its CEO, Jeffrey Immelt ($21.8 billion deficit); Boeing and its executive, Jim McNerney ($16.6 billion deficit); and AT&T and its CEO, Randall Stephenson ($10.2 billion deficit).[12] ExxonMobil, one of the world's largest companies, had a funding deficit of more than $10 billion as of 2011.[13] More than two-thirds of the five hundred companies that make up the S&P 500 have defined-benefit plans, and as of 2012 only eighteen of them were fully funded, according to the *New York Times*.[14] All told, the unfunded liabilities add up to around $355 billion, or about 22 percent of the funds' promised benefits.

Many labor union pension funds also are struggling, particularly in the aftermath of the Great Recession. A number of union pension funds are what's called "multiemployer plans," jointly sponsored by many employers and local or regional units of a labor union. At the end of 2008, 76 percent of union-backed multiemployer pension plans were safely solvent, but by 2009, after the crash, only 20 percent remained in the green zone. The rest had sunk into a yellow warning zone. The number of multiemployer plans projected to become insolvent has more than doubled. Nearly two hundred plans, or about 15 percent, are at risk of failure, potentially affecting nearly 2 million people. Those include the Central States Fund, the Teamsters' second-largest pension plan, and the United Mine Workers of America 1974 Pension Plan. Both are projected to run out of money in the next ten to twenty years unless they cut retirement benefits to members. The nation's largest multiemployer pension fund, the Western Conference of Teamsters Pension Fund with 583,000 participants, saw 28 percent of its pension assets wiped out by the financial crisis in 2008 (it has since recouped some of those losses).

Even the federal Pension Benefit Guaranty Corporation, which is the federal insurance backstop charged with bailing out struggling union pension funds, is in trouble. It has a $5.2 billion deficit and has booked liabilities of $7 billion dedicated to bailing out forty-nine insolvent multiemployer pension plans. An additional sixty-one plans have been terminated and will run out of money (and cease paying benefits to members) over the next few years, and forty-six more will terminate within the next decade.[15]

So both the private and public components of the US pension system have been on shaky ground for some time. The defined-benefit pension once provided a secure stream of retirement income on top of Social Security for many Americans, but in recent years the massive shortfalls in private and public pensions have become one of the great whispered secrets of modern politics. Nobody is quite sure what to do about it or how to build political consensus around a grand solution, so we just don't talk about it. Compared to these, Social Security is a model of financial sanity and stability.

The Cruel Hoax of 401(k)s and IRAs

During the Reagan era, private employers began walking away from their historical role as a mini–New Deal outpost providing pensions, health care, and other parts of the safety net for their employees. But have no fear America, said our nation's leaders: we have conjured up another means for providing retirement security. Enter the 401(k), along with its close cousins the 403(b) and the IRA.

Starting in the early 1980s, businesses began converting their company-sponsored defined-*benefit* plans to what became known as a defined-*contribution* plan, which meant the company would no longer pay a guaranteed monthly amount but would instead help collect your personal contributions into various tax-favored investments, such as a 401(k). It might seem obvious why companies would want to do that, given all the funding troubles that pensions began encountering in both the private and public sectors. Yet at the same time that companies were saying they could no longer afford defined-benefit pensions for their employees, they were paying increasingly astronomical salaries and bonus packages to their executives. Businesses were also receiving (and still receive) substantial federal deductions in the amount of a hundred billion dollars annually in return for providing their employees with pensions.[16] It's a matter of fiscal priorities, and where one chooses to spend the company profits produced by employees' labor and productivity. Nevertheless, the companies began winding down their company pensions and enrolling their employees instead in savings vehicles like 401(k)s, 403(b)s, IRAs, and the like. This turned out to be a disaster for most American workers, as well as the nation's retirement system.

The 401(k) and IRA vehicles were established by federal law in the late 1970s to allow workers to take part of their pay as tax-free deferred compensation. In the Revenue Act of 1978, Congress inserted a new section into the tax code, section 401(k), and prior to that, Individual Retirement Accounts (IRA) had been created as part of the 1974 Employee Retirement Income Security Act (ERISA). As for 403(b) accounts (tax-deferred accounts for employees of nonprofits), these have been around since the 1930s. But section 401(k) was the first provision that allowed workplace-sponsored retirement accounts that were fed by tax-deferred income for all types of employees. This opened the door for the proliferation of such accounts in the decades since.

A 401(k)-type plan is structured in a way that the architects believed would encourage Americans to save for their retirement. Just like with a pension, defined-contribution plans allow employees to have deducted from their pay on a voluntary basis a fixed amount of salary. That money can then be deposited into various types of investment vehicles, such as stocks and bonds, or into portfolios made up of various stocks and bonds, such as mutual funds. The more generous employers match a certain percentage of the employee's contribution to their retirement plan, but the contribution amount from the employer is much less than under a defined pension. The amount deducted from the employee's monthly salary is then subtracted from their gross wage when calculating taxable income, significantly lowering their tax burden. When I participated in such a plan through my employer, I socked away the maximum of around $22,000 per year and deposited that money into a bank account, mutual fund, or other investments. According to IRS rules, I was then allowed to deduct that $22,000 from my gross income, which meant I paid income tax on a much lower income, saving thousands of dollars (though because it's tax-*deferred*, I will have to pay taxes on that income once I retire, but by then my retirement income is likely to be lower, and so will be the income tax). By investing a chunk of my salary year after year in the stock market, it is assumed that several decades of investment income will expand my individual economic pie significantly. Another nice advantage of this method is that, unlike job-based pensions, the 401(k)s and IRAs are somewhat portable from job to job, so you don't have to worry about job-lock.

It can be a really great deal—but only if you earn enough income to participate. In an age of stagnant wages for most working Americans, therein lies a huge problem. Nearly half of all households have virtually no retirement savings. With incomes flat for the past several decades, who had extra money to save? You can't benefit from the tax-deferral of a 401(k) if you don't have any savings.

The decline in company pensions and the rise in 401(k)-type vehicles mirrored each other like the two ends of a seesaw. As the number of private pensions declined, the number of 401(k)s and IRAs dramatically increased. By 2011, the percentage of private-sector workers covered by company pensions had dropped from around 40 percent to 15 percent.[17] Yet at the same time, the number of businesses offering defined-contribution plans like 401(k)s soared. Since 1979, 401(k)-type retirement plans have gone from covering only about 17 percent of the private workforce to around 42 percent today.[18] Essentially these defined-contribution plans have taken over from traditional pensions.

Defined-contribution plans were hyped and sold to the American public as the new and improved successors to the guaranteed monthly payouts of a traditional pension. In actual fact, the 401(k) has been a dismal failure for a number of reasons. Besides most Americans not earning enough income to contribute much into these accounts, this type of private savings vehicle forces individuals to endure a number of significant risks, including:

Market risk. Unlike Social Security or the company's pension plan, a defined-contribution plan is not insurance—it is merely a tax-deferred savings account that can be invested in the stock market. A 401(k) puts all the risk upon the workers, who must decide how much to invest, and in which investments. Workers who have 401(k)s risk losing a chunk of their savings in a stock market downturn or crash, a particularly damaging prospect for workers nearing retirement.[19] Of course, this can happen to anyone who invests their money unwisely. In the case of a total stock market collapse, like what happened in 2000 and 2008, you can lose a lot of money if you invest anything at all. So switching from a defined-benefit plan to a defined-contribution plan has forced workers to assume a major amount of risk. Given stock market volatility in recent years, and the inherent gamble that investing in the stock market entails, the best investment strategy might be not to invest in the stock market at all. Because depending on when the next crash hits, you may be left holding the bag at the exact moment when you need that money for your retirement. In the financial crisis of 2008, individuals lost $2.8 trillion in the value of their 401(k) or IRA retirement plans.[20] That loss is equal to nearly a sixth of the size of the entire US economy.

Investment risk. In addition to the overall volatility of the market, 401(k)s force workers to manage their own investment portfolios, which often leads to lower-than-optimal performance for many reasons. Workers are not experienced stock market analysts and too often make the wrong decisions. They tend to hold undiversified portfolios, invest in too many high-risk stocks, and get impatient and/or spooked by market fluctuations and so buy and sell at the wrong time. Not surprisingly, most people generally lack the expertise necessary to earn high returns.[21]

Chris Farrell from *Bloomberg Business* says, "A cottage industry of behavioral economists has chronicled how poor most people are at making sound investment decisions. It's all too easy for employees to get caught up in market enthusiasms." Most people, he says, pile in just when prices are peaking and—when the market spooks—selling around a perceived market bottom. "Few get the hang of the differences between growth stocks and value stocks, let alone the key elements of diversification [and] asset allocation," says Farrell. "There's little time to learn modern portfolio money management."[22]

It's not just investment decisions that give most people difficulty. A study by the National Bureau of Economic Research found that more than one-quarter of baby boomer households thought "hardly at all" about retirement, and that financial literacy among boomers was "alarmingly low." About a third of households don't have a savings account, and more than 40 percent don't have enough savings to cover basic expenses if they lost their main source of income. Half the households could not do a simple math calculation (divide $2 million by five) and fewer than 20 percent could calculate compound interest.[23]

So, how could such individuals realistically be expected to oversee their own investment portfolio? Even many experienced mutual fund managers often fail to beat the performance of the stock market exchanges. Any retirement system that relies too much on the investing skill and acumen of the average person is destined to fail.

Contribution risk. Workers often contribute too little or too inconsistently to their accounts, so most are not able to accumulate a sufficient nest egg. Financial experts say it will take a monthly retirement income of about 70–80 percent of preretirement income levels—in addition to $200,000 to $300,000 in personal savings—for the average American to have a secure retirement.[24] Yet most older Americans have saved only a fraction of that. Three-quarters nearing retirement age have less than $30,000 in their retirement accounts, with one estimate from the National Institute on Retirement Security showing that a typical "near retirement household" has on average only $12,000 in "retirement account assets."[25] Retirement expert Alicia Munnell at the Center for Retirement Research has found that about half of all Americans are at risk of having insufficient retirement income, and three-fifths of low-income households are at risk of not having sufficient retirement income to maintain their preretirement standards of living (which, for poorer people, was already a low standard to begin with). All of these problems were exacerbated by the Great Recession.[26]

Longevity risk. Heaven forbid that it should be a liability that you might live too long. But for retirees who rely on their 401(k) to supplement Social Security, this is a real possibility. In their best-selling book *Get What's Yours: The Secret to Maxing Out Your Social Security*, experts Laurence Kotlikoff, Philip Moeller, and Paul Solman write that the greatest danger that retirees face is outliving their savings. They portray an old age in which the "golden years" have turned to lead, "weighed down by penury and its attendant anxieties."[27] That is a greater risk with a 401(k) or other type of defined-contribution plan, compared to a guaranteed payout pension plan (with a defined benefit), which lasts the rest of your life. Unquestionably, US workers were insured more efficiently and more securely under the traditional pension system. Without access to a company pension, many workers have become almost completely dependent on Social Security for their retirement needs.

Financial fees risk. Because most Americans do not have the expertise to know how to invest their savings, or the time to figure it out, many end up contracting with investment management firms that charge high account fees and take a big bite out of already-inadequate savings. As Yeva Nersisyan and L. Randall Wray have argued, the entire industry can be justified only if, through skill or luck, pension fund management can beat the average risk-free return on US treasuries by enough to pay for all of those industry compensations plus add growth to the fund portfolio.[28] Yet numerous studies have shown that the vast majority of professional managers don't realize higher stock market returns than what lead index funds like the Dow Jones Industrial average earns. There is no strong evidence that the typical fund manager can even consistently beat the average return on US treasuries. In other words, there is little expertise involved in performing no better than the stock market as a whole.

So even though it makes no economic sense to pay fees to financial managers, nevertheless the "hyper-individualized" nature of administration and management of millions of accounts generates excessive overhead costs that are ultimately absorbed by the workers themselves. By some estimates, these costs are more than twice as high as they would be under a more efficient retirement system.[29] Various reforms have been proposed, such as stricter regulations on brokers, disclosure of 401(k) fees, or requiring plan sponsors to offer lower-cost index funds. But those would fail to fix this fundamentally broken system. Fees would still remain high and workers would still be forced to shoulder most of the risks.

Welfare Plans for the Wealthy

Besides the increased risk and exposure to stock market fluctuations, defined-contribution plans like 401(k)s have fostered another appalling outcome that would be laughable if it wasn't so twisted—most of the tax-deferred subsidies have disproportionately benefited affluent Americans. Here's why.

As we have seen, individuals participating in 401(k)s, 403(b)s, and IRAs are allowed considerable tax deductions. These act to reduce the taxable income of only those people who are affluent enough to benefit from these savings instruments. Higher-income people take full advantage, and as a result they pay less tax on their reduced taxable income. Also, in some cases, they end up in a lower tax bracket and pay a lower tax rate. These advantages are mostly not available to the middle and working classes, and especially not to the poor, who rarely earn enough income to divert for savings or investment.

In 2012, the federal government spent over $165 billion subsidizing individual retirement savings, nearly 80 percent of which went to the top 20 percent of income earners.[30] Typically fewer than 30 percent of all filers even itemize deductions on their tax returns, which is necessary in order to receive a tax-deferred subsidy like a 401(k).[31] Again, the poor and middle classes rarely earn enough income to benefit from itemizing deductions. Only higher-income individuals earn enough to enjoy that luxury. Going forward, the nonpartisan Congressional Budget Office has calculated that from 2015 through 2024 the United States will spend $2.1 trillion subsidizing defined-contribution plans, most of which will benefit people in the top 20 percent income bracket.[32]

Social Security expert Philip Moeller agrees that the benefits of 401(k)s have been limited to higher-earning Americans. "The people who need the help the least are thus getting the lion's share of the tax benefits of these accounts, while half of the nation's workers can't even participate in a 401(k) and many of those who could simply do not make enough money to do so."[33]

No public interest justifies subsidies of private savings for the better-off through the tax code—yet that is exactly what current policy does. Nor is it sensible to have one of the three legs of the retirement stool dependent on several entirely unpredictable factors: how much discretionary funds one can stuff into these savings vehicles during your working life, which excludes those unlucky ones who don't earn enough income; how well the stock market performs over the life of the 401(k)/IRA, since that will determine its ultimate value; and how savvy the average person is at picking stock market winners. That just doesn't make sense, either from the perspective of retirees or of having a secure and stable retirement system. It only makes sense from the employer's perspective—shedding its obligation for providing company pensions and switching to 401(k)s was much less expensive and involved less risk for the company, and fewer potential headaches caused by fluctuations in stock and investment returns. Instead, all the risk was handed off to everyday American workers, most of whom are woefully ill equipped for such an undertaking.

It is important to emphasize that these risks and costs are an inherent part of the 401(k) system. So any reforms will have limited impact because the problem is endemic to a defined-contribution system where participants' success is dependent on an unpredictable stock market and their own ability to pick winners, and tax-deferred subsidies are provided to those who are already better off. Thus both the private and public components of the US employer-based retirement system are under severe strain, as the Great Recession—combined with prerecession patterns of rising inequality, stagnant wages, and a diminishing social contract—have taken their toll. We now have decades of data with which to assess the "defined-contribution revolution" from the 1970s, and we can unequivocally say that it has been a failure. It has shifted risks and costs onto everyday Americans who can least afford it, and it has failed to provide sufficient support for retirees.

With traditional company pensions covering fewer workers, and the remaining pensions on shaky ground, and with defined-contribution plans by definition riskier and more costly for employees, this leg of the three-legged retirement stool has been chopped back to the point where it is too short and unstable to contribute much to retirement well-being. It has led to more risk, more stock market gambling, and less guaranteed security.

The Second Failing Leg of Retirement Security: Homeownership and Private Savings

The second failing leg of the retirement system is based on individual asset ownership, and mostly is centered on homeownership. For tens of millions of Americans, security in their elderly years has been directly linked to the value of their homes. Yet the rupture of the housing bubble, which caused the value of homes across the country to collapse, illustrated the danger of over-reliance on home values for retirement security.

Homeowners lost approximately $8 trillion in value during the Great Recession, a 53 percent drop in the overall worth of the national homeownership stock.[34] Like our protagonists Howard and Jean, almost 10 million Americans—nearly a fifth of all homeowners—still remain "underwater" today, owing more on their mortgage than their home is worth, seven years after the housing collapse.[35] That number is even higher—30 percent—

among those owning low-price homes. According to *Forbes*, more than one-third of all homeowners with a mortgage are "effectively" underwater, meaning they have less than 20 percent equity in their home. These homeowners are for the most part flat broke if they have no other accumulated savings or retirement vehicle (which, as we have seen, most don't have).

Prior to the housing collapse in 2008, only the top 50 percent of income earners had accumulated enough wealth from financial assets and pensions to weather the bursting housing bubble, when the value of homes took a nosedive by 40 percent or more. The bottom 50 percent had not saved enough beyond their homeownership to avoid severe wreckage to their retirement plans when their homes' worth plummeted. This was devastating for Americans' retirement well-being because, with the rate of homeownership in the United States being 65 percent of all households (before the housing bubble collapse in 2008 it was nearly 70 percent), this accounts for a large proportion of the assets owned by a large portion of the population.[36]

Besides homeownership, many people also have some degree of non-home assets in the form of private savings. But for most Americans, their level of private savings is too low to serve even as a personal buffer against sudden hard times, let alone as the basis of a secure retirement. *New York Times* columnist Paul Krugman reported about a household survey conducted by the US Federal Reserve in 2015, which found that "47 percent [of households] said that they do not have the resources to meet an unexpected expense of $400," and "would have to sell something or borrow to meet that need." Only $400! More than three in ten Americans reported going without some kind of medical care in the past year because they couldn't afford it, and the same number have no retirement savings or pension.[37] These 132.1 million "liquid asset poor" Americans include many members of the middle class: more than a quarter of households earning between $55,465 and $90,000 per year have less than three months of liquid savings.[38]

Complicating matters, the lack of private savings has weakened the other legs of the retirement stool. More than one in four households has had to withdraw savings from their 401(k) or

403(b) retirement accounts before retirement to pay for an emergency. These early withdrawals totaled $60 billion out of a total of $176 billion (40 percent) contributed by employees to defined contribution accounts in 2010, even though early withdrawals come with heavy penalty fees.[39] With defined-contribution plans already insufficient to cover retirement needs, the lack of private savings to cover sudden personal emergencies has made the problem much worse.

There is one other disturbing aspect about using homeownership as a personal piggy bank. As with the federally subsidized 401(k)s and IRAs, the United States provides substantial subsidies for homeowners through vehicles like the home mortgage interest deduction, a deduction for state and local property taxes, a lower capital gains tax rate on home sales, and other home-related deductions. These are meant to encourage homeownership-based retirement. Yet here, too, the homeownership deductions are upside down—they primarily benefit well-to-do Americans, even though these are the people who need assistance the least.

The federal subsidy for the home mortgage interest deduction amounts to around $70 billion per year, and a lopsided 86 percent of the home mortgage interest deductions in 2014 went to those people in the top 10 percent income bracket.[40] Then there's also a federal tax deduction for state and local property taxes paid on one's home that cost the federal budget another $32 billion in 2014.[41] And adding insult to injury, homeowners also do not have to pay taxes on up to $250,000 of capital gains when they sell their primary residence, which doubles to $500,000 for married taxpayers; that capital gains exclusion cost the government about $52 billion in 2014 and almost exclusively benefited the rich.[42] Together, these three housing tax expenditures totaled an astonishing $154 billion in 2014—and they primarily benefited higher-income Americans.[43] So, only a small minority of people benefit from these policies. Renters and most low-income people don't benefit at all. If the mortgage interest deduction were banished from planet Earth, most middle- or working-class Americans would see no negative impact on their taxes because it already doesn't involve them.

In comparison, the US Department of Housing and Urban Development, which administers the government's largest affordable housing programs for low-income people, spent barely a quarter of that $154 billion, about $42 billion in 2014.[44] In addition, over a third of the nation's households are renters, yet they received less than one-fourth of all federal housing subsidies; three-quarters of federal housing expenditures in 2012 went to homeowners (with a disproportionate amount of that benefiting wealthier Americans). Overall, the Center on Budget and Policy Priorities found that the 5 million households with incomes of $200,000 or more received a larger share of federal spending on housing than the more than 20 million households with incomes of $20,000 or less—even though lower-income families are far more likely to struggle with finding affordable housing.[45]

Treating homeownership as a core part of the retirement stool, and then providing deductions, exclusions, and deferrals for homeowners through the tax code, has turned out to cause massive subsidies to flow to the upper 10 percent of wealthy Americans. Yet these people in fact don't need help nearly as much as the bottom 90 percent of Americans. So this second leg of the three-legged retirement stool—homeownership and private savings—has proven to be as weak and unreliable as employer pensions and 401(k)s. In our upside-down system, the higher one's income the greater the value of the tax subsidies offered. The current retirement system finances upper-income people at the expense of middle- and working-class Americans who can least afford homeownership or private retirement savings. The tax code has created a two-tier welfare state in which wealthier people enjoy generous tax deductions as incentives to encourage homeownership and personal savings. While a couple of decades ago it seemed like a good idea to deploy the tax code for that purpose, at this point it's clear that the tax system has become so turned on its head that it's better-off Americans who are today's "welfare queens," not the poor.

A phasing out of these various loopholes, and gradually reducing the amount of private income that wealthier people can shelter from taxation, would result in increased revenue available to convert Social Security into a more robust and expanded platform (in chapter 5, I will explore various ways to pay for a doubling of the Social Security payout, especially targeting the tax rules that shelter high-income households and businesses from paying their fair share; can you say "step-up in basis"?). Far from hurting the economy, reducing these tax advantages for the better-off would not only be more fair, but it would help the economy in a number of ways, including contributing toward an expansion of Social Security that would have a stimulating effect on the entire national economy.

With private-sector employers walking away from their traditional role of providing a pension; and with the decline of unions, which is correlated with the decline of pensions in both the public and private sectors; and with chronic volatility in the stock and housing markets, and an over-reliance on 401(k)s and homeownership as part of our national retirement system, two of the three legs have been sawed back to nubs. The retirement stool is no longer stable or secure, and consequently the retirement prospects for most Americans have deteriorated. In the decades ahead, the vast majority of baby boomers and other retirees will be almost completely dependent on the third leg—the single remaining leg—of Social Security for their retirement.

The Third (Surviving) Leg of Retirement Security: Social Security

Where would the nation's retirees be without Social Security? At this point, most Americans have internalized the collapse of the two legs of the retirement stool; everybody knows it has happened, even if we don't talk about it. It's become the new normal. While Social Security was originally conceived back in the Great Depression of the 1930s as a mere retirement supplement, it has now come full circle to be the country's de facto national retirement system for most Americans—the last leg standing. Thankfully, despite what so many of its critics say, Social Security is on pretty solid financial ground. The Congressional Budget Office projects that Social Security can pay all scheduled benefits out of its own dedicated tax revenue stream through at least 2033 (after that, it will be able to pay 75 percent of benefits, assuming no other reforms are enacted). The reason why is because Social Security has its own dedicated funding source, and every working American sees evidence of that on every paycheck in the form of a 6.2 percent deduction from their checks (with employers matching that). Contrary to what so many critics say, Social Security has not added a penny to the federal budget deficit, indeed it has been running *surpluses*. No other government program except Medicare can claim it is fully funded with dedicated revenue for the next twenty years.

So, Social Security is not "going broke," not by a long shot. That sound bite is just the static put out by its critics to spread F-U-D—fear, uncertainty, and doubt. The bigger problem with the US retirement system is that, with the sawing off of the other two legs of the retirement stool, Social Security has become our country's de facto national retirement plan. Despite that criticality, its payout is relatively meager, certainly too meager to play such a central role. Currently it replaces 30–40 percent of a worker's average wage at retirement (other countries with more robust national pensions provide twice the US replacement rate). That income is simply not enough to live on when it is your primary—perhaps your only—source of retirement income.

That's why this book will make the case that, rather than cutting Social Security, we should expand it. In fact, we should *double* the individual payout for the 43 million Americans who annually receive individual retirement benefits.

But as we will see in the next chapter, rather than talking about expanding Social Security, the politicians in Washington, DC, are talking about cutting it. Bizarrely, the only bipartisan proposal currently under consideration calls for—not 401(k) overhaul, or raising the payroll cap, or a rethinking of homeownership as a retirement foundation—but *cuts to the last remaining leg of Social Security*. It's a stunning failure of our nation's politics and politicians, and of our collective imagination. It's a failure of our national *ideology*, which is blinded by an allegiance to outdated ways of thinking.

For more and more Americans, the dream of a secure retirement is standing on a single wobbly leg, trying to stand upright as the ground beneath continues to shake. With the three-legged stool nearly collapsed for most people, the current cohort of seniors may turn out to be the last generation of well-off and secure retirees that the United States will ever see. Labor economist Teresa Ghilarducci spells out what's at stake: "Policy makers and leaders can and must find a way to save retirement, a necessary—and now threatened—feature of civilized societies."[46]

CHAPTER THREE

The Bipartisan Attack on Retirement Security

The debate over the US retirement system, including Social Security, is a debate over what kind of society we want to live in. Opinion polls continue to show that a large super majority of Americans—Democrats, independents, and Republicans alike—support Social Security, oppose cuts to benefits, oppose privatization, think everyone should pay their fair share, and would pay higher taxes to sustain it.[1] Yet the elite in Washington, DC, including many think tanks, policy experts, influential pundits, news media, congressional staffers, Republican and Democratic politicians, inexplicably continue to call for cutbacks in the false name of fiscal responsibility.

As attempts since the Reagan era to unravel key cornerstones of the New Deal have unfolded, including the extreme deregulation of the banking and financial industry which directly led to the economic collapse in 2008, it is hardly surprising that the architects of austerity have also waged a war to undercut Social Security. What is more surprising, however, is that, given the overwhelming popularity of Social Security, this Ayn Rand brand of libertarianism has made so much progress in its backward-looking project of privatizing the retirement system.

The Republican Party today is a different species than when

Social Security booster Dwight Eisenhower was president. Eisenhower left office in 1960, but within just a few years the Grand Old Party launched itself in a radically new direction. Barry Goldwater, the Republican nominee for president in 1964, led the cavalry's charge with what was to become a frequent conservative rallying cry, later popularized by Ronald Reagan. Goldwater said, "I have little interest in streamlining government or in making it more efficient, for I mean to reduce its size. I do not undertake to promote welfare, for I propose to extend freedom. My aim is not to pass laws, but to repeal them. It is not to inaugurate new programs, but to cancel old ones that . . . impose on the people an unwarranted financial burden."[2]

That was the beginning of a new era for the party of Lincoln, a transmogrification that was fully realized with the election of Reagan in 1980. From that point forward, most Republican leaders have strategically attacked government programs that actually help people as part of their smackdown of government itself. This relentless, well-planned and well-funded assault has served to undermine American's faith in our own institutions of self-rule. Conservatives' obsession over killing Social Security is precisely driven by their recognition that the program's popularity helps legitimize government in the eyes of the public. Stephen Moore, the chief economist at the right-wing Heritage Foundation, once proclaimed that Social Security is "the soft underbelly of the welfare state" and if activists could "jab your spear through that" they could slay the sacred cow.[3]

But when programs are too popular to attack directly, like Medicare or Social Security, Republicans have taken to undermining them by feigning a principled concern about debt, deficits, and our ability to pay. Yet that concern is opportunistic and largely fictitious. After all, when Mitt Romney and Wisconsin representative Paul Ryan were the GOP's presidential and vice presidential standard-bearers in the 2012 election, they proposed a 20 percent cut in income tax rates, plus other tax cuts that would have added about $6 trillion to the deficit over ten years. They also proposed increased military spending that would have added another $2 trillion to the nation's debt. That lack of concern over increased deficits and debt did not raise any concerns among the GOP faithful. Many Republicans only seem to be concerned about debt when they are criticizing government expenditures of which they don't approve. But when it comes to spending for their preferred national priorities, Republicans are willing to spend tax dollars like drunken sailors on a port o' call spree.

To be fair, the Romney-Ryan ticket claimed it could implement its tax cuts for the wealthy, as well as their other preferred expenditure increases, without adding to the national debt load. They boasted that their changes to the nation's fiscal and tax priorities would be "revenue neutral," allowing Republicans to dodge the charge that they were being hypocritical. But the dodge was only superficial, since the Romney-Ryan budget was full of funny math that did not hold up even to the most elementary scrutiny. We have seen thirty years of evidence that tax cuts directed at the wealthy not only do not pay for themselves, but they also do not correlate with higher economic growth. The *Wall Street Journal* reported on a study from the National Bureau of Economic Research, which found that tax cuts aimed at the wealthy do not spur growth in output and jobs, nor do they eventually trickle down to the masses, because it turns out that the wealthy tend to save the money rather than invest it.[4] Yet people believe what they want to believe, and the millions of Americans who voted for the Romney-Ryan ticket apparently were untroubled by the prospect of even larger deficits, as long as they served their partisan interests and priorities.

Flash forward to the field of Republican presidential candidates for the 2016 election. With seventeen political and business leaders tossing their hats into the ring, candidate after candidate expressed what the *US News & World Report* called "unwavering fealty to a failed theory" of trickle-down economics.[5] This included US senator Rand Paul's proposal for a flat tax—elimination of the progressive income tax, another New Deal achievement—and Senator Marco Rubio's tax cuts for the wealthy based on the total elimination of capital gains and dividends taxes, which would almost exclusively benefit the wealthy and be far larger than the massive tax cuts enacted by President

George W. Bush. The always provocative former Texas governor Rick Perry, who eventually pulled out of the race, has called Social Security "a Ponzi scheme," as has Texas Senator Ted Cruz.[6]

Many pundits and political analysts have wondered why, given the popularity of Social Security even among the Republican base, these GOP leaders try to row so hard in the opposite direction. According to *New York Times* columnist Paul Krugman, "This apparent act of political self-destructiveness probably reflects an attempt to curry favor with wealthy donors."[7] In a separate piece, Krugman hammered on this theme, saying, "The invisible primary has been reduced to a stark competition for the affections and, of course, the money of a few dozen plutocrats."[8] The only candidates who raised a dissenting voice against those bashing Social Security and entitlements were Donald Trump and Mike Huckabee, who criticized the Republican chorus for betraying America's seniors. *Vox*'s Ezra Klein observed, "Both parties [are] vulnerable to a candidate like Trump who has the money, and the star power, to campaign on a platform that party elites would normally suppress."[9]

Indeed, if he had been elected president, Mitt Romney's proposals would have amounted to a continuation of a longtime conservative philosophy called "starve the beast." Conservatives have long had a strategy of actually provoking a deficit "crisis" by way of government shutdowns and other tactics so that the crisis can be solved by raising the pressure to cut government programs that Republicans don't like. In the words of notorious GOP operative and antitax crusader Grover Norquist—taking his cue from Barry Goldwater—"I don't want to abolish government. I simply want to reduce it to the size where I can drag it into the bathroom and drown it in the bathtub."[10]

In the Crosshairs of a Billionaire's Obsession

So Romney and Ryan's talk about "revenue neutral" was simply electioneering pixie dust to fool independent and swing voters who did not have the time or the inclination to subject their claims to sufficient scrutiny. Their campaign was just the latest point of the spear for conservative organizations and leaders who had long advocated cutting or privatizing entitlements. Chief among those has been conservative Wall Street billionaire Peter G. Peterson, who was briefly secretary of commerce in the Nixon administration, and then became CEO of Lehman Brothers (which later collapsed during the financial crisis of 2008), and later a cofounder of the private equity firm Blackstone Group. He is also former chairman of the Federal Reserve Bank of New York.

Even by billionaire standards, Peter G. Peterson is no ordinary plutocrat. The *Los Angeles Times*'s Pulitzer Prize–winning reporter Michael Hiltzik has called Peterson "the most influential billionaire in America," more influential than George Soros or the Koch brothers, Charles and David.

Peterson "isn't content merely to express concern about the federal deficit," Hiltzik says. "His particular targets are Social Security, Medicare and Medicaid, which he calls 'entitlement' programs and which he wants to cut back in a manner that would strike deeply at the middle class."[11]

Peterson's billions have backed a large number of think tanks, including the Concord Coalition, formed to "fix the nation's debt problem" and "unsustainable entitlement programs," as well as the Campaign to Fix the Debt, the Committee for a Responsible Federal Budget, and, most importantly, his very own Peter G. Peterson Foundation (which he launched in 2008). These organizations and others champion his pet causes, and take his fiscal austerity message outside the Beltway. He has sprinkled his donations around to numerous organizations and candidates on both sides of the aisle, launching TV ad campaigns to push his debt politics and starting his own media outlet called the *Fiscal Times* to churn out articles about fiscal issues. He even funded a college and high school campaign called "Up to Us," ostensibly aimed at "teaching kids about the national debt," but in fact it was targeted at fomenting a generational war between young people and seniors over Social Security. In essence, Peterson, a fabulously wealthy and consummate Wall Street insider, has bankrolled his own movement over the past thirty years, and Social Security is squarely in his crosshairs.

Peterson says his concern is over a government drowning in

debt, particularly in the aftermath of the government bailout of Wall Street and the economy after the 2008 collapse. But economist Dean Baker, codirector of the Center for Economic and Policy Research, disputes this. "He's not focused on the debt so much as on cutting Social Security and Medicare," Baker says. "Even in the late '90s, when we had a surplus, he was saying the same thing and the debt wasn't in any obvious way a problem then."[12]

Peterson has shown a deftness at making his views and actions seem nonpartisan and even mainstream, and he has been able to influence both Beltway Republicans and Democrats to the point where "urgent reform" of Social Security and Medicare has become a foundation of a bipartisan consensus. Yet, Hiltzik explains, "Peterson's evidence can be misleading and his contentions questionable. The avoidance of overt *political* partisanship enables Peterson to engage in something more insidious: *economic* partisanship." In the battle over Social Security we see the familiar pattern of the rich and powerful against nearly everyone else, the 1 percent versus the 99 percent.

But Peterson does not make those sorts of class-based arguments head-on. Instead, he has argued that too much entitlement money is going to the middle class, and that cutting off payments to these recipients "would balance the budget, and would do so with a comfortable surplus to spare." Cleverly, he even tries to overturn the class warfare card by claiming that "a substantial part" of retirement payments go to wealthy people like him, and that this is a waste of money and national resources. But in fact, Social Security payments to recipients earning annual incomes of $1 million or more typically amount to peanuts—seventeen-hundredths of 1 percent (yes, 0.17 percent)—of all benefits paid out.

"The hallmark of Peterson's worldview," Hiltzik says, "is to view social insurance programs such as Social Security and Medicare strictly as fiscal expense items, ignoring their roots as moral commitments to American citizens that cross generations and unite economic classes." Portraying them, as Peterson does, as "safety net" initiatives that should only be available for the most destitute Americans reconceptualizes Social Security and Medicare as welfare for the poor, rather than as an insurance program into which workers have contributed premiums all their working lives. Peterson and his allies are quite consciously trying to undermine the universal appeal of these popular programs. Yet Peterson has managed to sell his soap to the point where his views dominate Beltway discussions over Social Security and so-called entitlements. "The shame of Washington," Hiltzik adds, is that almost every organization allegedly trying to "fix" these programs "has accepted, somewhere and somehow, money from Pete Peterson."[13]

Peterson's ambitious efforts sometimes have resorted to exaggeration, hyperbole, and even fakery. He and his allies deployed a favorite tactic of campaigning for benefit cuts to Social Security by blending Social Security with Medicare's future trend lines. Unquestionably, the cost of health care has exploded in the United States and threatens to undermine the nation's finances. But when opponents like Peterson criticize the costs of "entitlements," nearly all of those costs come from Medicare (though Medicare costs are a good bargain compared to the exorbitant, privatized US health-care system, which is twice as expensive as health-care systems in other developed nations). By lumping together Medicare and Social Security into "entitlements," the critics are using a meat cleaver approach instead of a scalpel in their bid to call for severe cuts to both.

Peterson also spent a lot of money to organize a charade of town hall meetings to advance his agenda. The Peterson Foundation reportedly gave over $2 million to America Speaks, one of the leading innovators in the field of public deliberative democracy, to organize nineteen town hall meetings across the country.[14] With the digital magic of the Internet and video capabilities, these nineteen locations were all linked together simultaneously, on the same day in June 2010. It was billed as "Internet democracy at its most sophisticated," showing the capabilities of this live crowdsourcing technology. All told, more than 3,500 average Americans from across the country were summoned to deliberate on the "debt problem." At the town halls, participants were provided "objective" information about the problem, as well as potential solutions.

But the objective information turned out to have been

Peterson-ified in advance. *Salon* financial columnist David Dayen reported that "the entire event was absolutely designed to create a panic about the deficit among the participants. Slickly produced scare videos talking about the dire straits of the budget were prevalent. Multiple charts and graphs without precise numbers or percentages were handed out." One video featured deficit hawk Rep. Paul Ryan, as well as Federal Reserve Chair and former Bush Council of Economic Advisors chair Ben Bernanke. President Barack Obama was also featured in the video. "The speakers, and the content," Dayen wrote, "seemed skewed" in favor of one side of the argument.[15]

Through the wizardry of modern digital communications, the 3,500 participants at the America Speaks town halls all watched and listened at the same time, a virtual high-tech "national town hall meeting." But at the Los Angeles location, things didn't go as scripted. In the words of Thomas Frank, author of *What's the Matter with Kansas*, "They deliberated, and then something funny happened on the way to the consensus."[16] Instead of participants coming to the conclusion that had been planned, that debt and deficits were evil and Social Security and other entitlements had to be cut in order to save them—a "we have to burn the village in order to save it" mentality—the Angelenos in attendance tore up the script. Instead they wound up supporting "an extra 5 percent tax" on incomes of greater than $1 million per year (by 68 percent), an increase in the corporate income tax rate (59 percent), and a "securities transactions tax" (61 percent) as alternative ways to close the deficit and fund entitlements. Specifically on Social Security, a whopping 85 percent supported raising the limit on the payroll tax so that all income levels pay the same rate of Social Security tax as a means of stabilizing the retirement system. Despite the scaremongering and factual distortions they encountered, these Americans spoke, loudly and clearly, about their opposition to rolling back Social Security and Medicare.

The Party of FDR Goes AWOL
It's clear that the Republican Party is no longer the party of Ike Eisenhower, and it's a foregone conclusion that the GOP and

its leaders are antigovernment and against all forms of what are today referred to as "entitlements." At this point, it is in their partisan DNA. But what about the Democrats? What explains their transmutation, from the party of Franklin Roosevelt and the New Deal that launched Social Security—one of the most popular government programs of all time—to a party that also now appears to hold a meat cleaver, ready to chop away at one of the foundations of the US middle class?

As a candidate for president, Barack Obama first raised some liberal and progressive eyebrows with his Peterson-like take on Social Security. Obama invoked the GOP talking point about the "Social Security crisis"[17]—which, as we saw in chapter 1, doesn't really exist except in the minds of those who want to cut it. And then as president-elect he pledged in January 2009, just before assuming office, in a meeting with the *Washington Post* editorial board, to enact reforms to fix the alleged crisis.[18] His solutions have included various ways to cut benefits. For example, Obama has promoted an alternative measurement of the consumer price index known as the "chained CPI," which, if used, would amount to a less-generous annual rate of increase for Social Security payments and federal-employee retirement annuities. Under Obama's plan, a seventy-three-year-old retiree would see a 2.5 percent reduction in Social Security payments, which by the age of ninety-three would balloon to a 7.2 percent cut in her or his Social Security payments. Obama only dropped this idea after a massive outcry from many Democrats and progressives.[19]

Hillary Clinton also has been slippery on Social Security, and in some ways worse than Obama. She has a long track record of waffling and fudging on the subject of what to do about entitlements. In the 2008 Democratic presidential primary debate in Philadelphia, Clinton was asked if she would agree to lift the Social Security payroll cap on individuals making more than the then upper limit of $97,000 per year so that wealthier people would pay a fairer share into the Trust Fund. In the debate, Obama correctly stated, "Right now millionaires and billionaires don't have to pay beyond $97,000 a year." To this, Clinton responded blandly, "I don't want to raise taxes on anybody," and made a feeble defense of why it was OK that the wealthy paid a lower percentage of their income toward Social Security than the rest of Americans.[20] In a debate in Las Vegas, she called Barack Obama's proposal to lift the payroll cap a trillion-dollar increase "on middle class families"—despite the fact that (at the time) only 6 percent of Americans made over $97,000 per year.[21]

Flash forward to October 2016, when she visited New Hampshire as part of her presidential run. Clinton again tried to stoke fear over hurting "middle class families" as she refused to endorse lifting the payroll cap.[22] Yet the Center for Economic Policy and Research found that a mere 6 percent of the richest Americans (just over 9 million people) earned more than the $118,500 taxable limit.[23] In New Hampshire Clinton also would not categorically rule out making cuts to Social Security benefits or raising the retirement age. Earlier in the campaign, Clinton did at least say that Republican candidates' proposals to "privatize" or "undermine" Social Security are "just wrong." But when her campaign was asked if she supported expanding Social Security, or if she favored some of the Republican presidential candidates' other proposals, such as raising the retirement age or means-testing, her campaign spokesman did the Hillary dodge, saying only that "dealing with challenges facing older Americans is a top priority for her."[24]

Besides Clinton presenting herself as a protector of the middle class in such an obviously disingenuous way, she has also delivered speeches, for which she has been lucratively paid, to employees of the controversial investment bank Goldman Sachs (particularly irksome since Lloyd Blankfein, CEO of Goldman Sachs, has proclaimed to CBS News that "entitlements" must be "contained"). All of this has only fostered deep suspicion about her true beliefs and values. It certainly did not endear her to the progressive and liberal wings of the Democratic Party. Clinton's unreliability on Social Security, Medicare, and other entitlements caused many progressives to grumble that she should not simply be automatically coronated with the presidential nomination, and became one of the crucial motivators for US senator Bernie Sanders from Vermont to throw his hat into the ring.

But this lack of FDR-ness, or even JFK-ness "profiles in courage" on the part of leading Democrats, is nothing new. Many people forget that President Bill Clinton negotiated with Republican House Speaker Newt Gingrich over a plan to "save" Social Security that included partial privatization.[25] That grand bargain imploded under the weight of the Monica Lewinsky scandal and Clinton's impeachment, but Clinton's willingness to "go there" caused lasting harm because no Democratic president had ever before agreed that there was a Social Security "crisis" that needed to be "solved." Clinton's decision provided political cover for politicians of both parties, as well as for special interests like the billionaire Pete Peterson, to advance schemes for restructuring the program.

That in turn led directly to President George W. Bush's Commission to Strengthen Social Security, which in fact was a commission trying to *privatize* Social Security by way of individual accounts—an odd way to strengthen it by in effect wiping it out. So when President Barack Obama took office, the public discourse was already a punishing one. The Bush privatization plan was defeated, but nevertheless President Obama, who was elected twice by voters who overwhelmingly support Social Security, appointed his National Commission on Fiscal Responsibility and Reform in February 2010, with a charge of drafting a plan to "balance the budget . . . and address the growth of entitlement spending." It sounded like a fiscally responsible thing to do, but a big red flag warned of trouble ahead when he appointed his cochairs: the conservative North Carolina Democrat Erskine Bowles and the conservative Republican Alan Simpson.

The two were charged with the task of forging a "bipartisan" plan, yet both were known to be no friends of Social Security or Medicare. Like Pete Peterson, Bowles also had deep ties to Wall Street and the financial industry, including being on the board of directors of investment bank Morgan Stanley (which received a $107 billion bailout from the Federal Reserve when it was on the brink of collapse in 2008, according to *Bloomberg Business*).[26] And the colorfully blunt Simpson had helped popularize the term "greedy geezers" to describe retired elderly who were allegedly stealing from young people; previously he had described Social

Security as "a milk cow with 310 million tits."[27] Both Bowles and Simpson became leaders in Peterson's group Campaign to Fix the Debt, which targeted Social Security for "reforms."

The Simpson-Bowles Commission, as it came to be called, was marred by controversy and headlines from the get-go, and the commission never released an official report because too many of its members disagreed with the strongly held opinions of Simpson and Bowles. But the cochairs went rogue and issued their own report in December 2010, calling for federal budget cuts and reductions to Social Security benefits by raising the retirement age, by means testing (which would undermine the universality of the program), and reducing the cost-of-living adjustments by adopting the chained CPI (and on Medicare, they called for making seniors pay higher premiums). Despite the lack of agreement among the members of the Simpson-Bowles Commission, and widespread opposition within his own party, President Obama inexplicably proposed in his second term a reduction of benefits by moving to incorporate into his 2014 budget the chained CPI cost-of-living formula. This move was fiercely opposed by Social Security advocates, both inside and outside the Democratic Party.

The Democrats have become dominated by Obama and Clinton strategists who, although they still believe in government involvement in the economy (more than Republicans), also advocate for so-called free market "solutions" to a range of problems. But increasingly their arguments stretch the boundaries of common sense, and do nothing to address the unfairness of the status quo. As we have seen, billions of dollars in federal taxes are spent subsidizing the private savings and retirement plans, as well as the homeownership, of the top 10 percent of income earners. Meanwhile, everyone else is left scrambling in this increasingly "ownership"—that is, "on your own"—society. And Democratic administrations and majorities in Congress have done little to stop it.

The Four Musketeers—Er, Social Security Commissions—to the Rescue

We can track what has happened to the Democratic Party on this issue by looking at the four Social Security commissions that were established over the last five decades, practically one every decade. It seems like just about every president has felt compelled to set up a commission to "save" Social Security. It has become a crucial wedge issue that the politicians toss in the air when they need to, like a political football that adds the right amount of misdirection to their overall agenda.

The first and most important of these four commissions was the National Commission on Social Security Reform, also known as the Greenspan Commission because its chairman was Alan Greenspan, who later was appointed chairman of the US Federal Reserve. It was established by the US Congress and President Ronald Reagan in 1981 to study and make recommendations regarding a short-term financing crisis that Social Security faced at that time. Reagan had never been a strong supporter of Social Security; indeed, he wanted to privatize it, and in 1975 had suggested making Social Security voluntary and letting workers make their own investments in the stock market.[28] But by the early 1980s Social Security had become what was known as the "third rail of politics," a reference to the high-voltage subway rail that powers the trains—"anyone who tries to touch it gets electrocuted."[29]

Estimates at the time found that the Social Security Trust Fund would run out of money as early as August 1983. President Reagan's executive order outlined the Greenspan Commission's mission as one of devising policy interventions "that will both assure the financial integrity of the Social Security System and the provision of appropriate benefits." In a letter to congressional leaders dated July 18, 1981, the president wrote, "The highest priority of my Administration is restoring the integrity of the Social Security System. Those 35 million Americans who depend on Social Security expect and are entitled to prompt bipartisan action to resolve the current financial problem."[30] As Social Security experts Nancy Altman and Eric Kingson have observed, unlike in today's debates, President Reagan didn't include anything in his executive order about balanced budgets or government debt and deficits, and certainly no mention of the dreaded word "entitlements."

Instead, the Greenspan Commission focused like a laser on Social Security solely, making sure that its dedicated funding from the payroll tax would be sufficient to provide the desired level of benefits for decades to come. Commission members wisely excluded Medicare from their mission because they understood that Medicare was substantially different from Social Security, requiring different expertise and solutions. Including Medicare along with Social Security undoubtedly would have made the politics of figuring out a remedy for both of them a lot more complex.[31] If the commission was serious about finding a bipartisan patch to a short-term funding shortfall for Social Security, it made a lot of sense to take this narrow approach.

Indeed, the Greenspan Commission's very first recommendation to Congress was that it "should not alter the fundamental structure of the Social Security program or undermine its fundamental principles."[32] The commissioners displayed a serious commitment to this very popular, pragmatic, and useful federal program, and its final report led to the Social Security Reform Act of 1983. That legislation fixed the short-term problem by increasing the payroll tax a bit, and it addressed long-term funding issues by gradually raising the retirement age from sixty-five to sixty-seven. It wasn't a perfect solution, as it required a tax increase that was going to disproportionately impact the middle and working classes, and an increase in the retirement age did amount to a benefit cut. But bipartisan consensus was achieved in a way that preserved the best features of this crucial retirement and antipoverty program for decades to come. In the annals of government policymaking, the Greenspan Commission enjoys a reputation as a successful model of bipartisanship and effectiveness.

But just a decade later, President Bill Clinton appointed another commission—the Bipartisan Commission on Entitlement and Tax Reform, chaired by Senators Bob Kerrey (Democrat) and John Danforth (Republican). For the first time, in the very title of the commission itself, the dreaded word "entitlement" now had entered the nation's lexicon. Altman and Kingson (who had been staffers for the Reagan commission, and Kingson for the Clinton commission) point out that never before had a commission lumped together Social Security, Medicare, and Medicaid as part of a "unified entitlement crisis." It made no sense, from the point of view of sincerely grappling with any emerging challenges, but it was a smart political move on the part of Social Security's opponents to stuff them all into the same bag in their attempt to drown them all.

That's because Medicare and Medicaid, the health-care programs for seniors and the disabled, really do suffer from potential bankruptcy challenges going forward due to the outlandishly high costs of health care in the United States, whether in the private or public sectors (the United States pays approximately twice as much money per capita for health care, for less coverage of our overall population, compared to other developed nations). In less than a year, as Altman and Kingson explain in their book, *Social Security Works!*, the eleven-letter word "entitlements" went from being "perfectly respectable budget jargon into the proverbial four-letter word, used to suggest that the benefits Americans had and were earning were less than deserved."[33]

The commission deadlocked on its recommendations, with not a single policy remedy receiving a majority of commission member votes, and little of its ambitious agenda was ever implemented. Nevertheless, this commission, which had been established by a Democratic president, did more than any other previous body to stigmatize the term "entitlement," and determined the terms and context of the debate for years to come. Many news media outlets aided and abetted this wayward process, blaring front-page headlines about the alleged problems caused by allegedly out-of-control entitlement spending. Clinton's Entitlement Commission was also noteworthy due to the participation of one of its members: billionaire Peter G. Peterson, who was to continue pushing his opposition agenda and play a prominent role in the entitlement debate for the next twenty years.

With the mischievous genie let out of the bottle by Clinton's Entitlement Commission, the stage was set for a serious assault on the people's fortress of Social Security. All the effort needed was a sympathetic president willing to use his office as a bully pulpit for the cause. Enter, President George W. Bush.

President Bush upped the ante—not only did he support cutting back Social Security, but he made the privatization of Social Security a centerpiece of his domestic agenda in his second term. In his 2005 State of the Union address, and in subsequent speeches he made touring the country to promote his plan, President Bush preached the familiar mantra that Social Security was "created decades ago, for a very different era." Now the system was outdated and in need of modernization, he said, and going broke besides. President Bush spread deceptive untruths, stating that Social Security's reserves were only IOUs, practically worthless paper backed by no real assets, and that future benefits might not be honored. He tried to sow generational discord by pitting younger workers against the elderly, saying that overly generous senior benefits were pickpocketing from younger Americans.

As his "solution," President Bush pushed a plan for privatization of this jewel of the New Deal. His plan included allowing young workers to keep some of their Social Security contributions and stash them into individual private accounts that could be invested in the stock market. He smiled out of both sides of his face, calling Social Security "one of the greatest achievements of the American government, and one of the deepest commitments to the American people,"[34] even as he pushed his privatization plans that would have destroyed it. Indeed, George W. Bush called his commission the 2001 President's Commission to Strengthen Social Security, yet he and his strategists plotted to weaken it. This was the moment for which many of Social Security's opponents had waited decades.

Keep in mind, privatization would have meant steering the $2.8 trillion Social Security Trust Fund into private accounts for individual Americans, who then would have had little choice but to invest their private security account into the stocks and bonds markets if they wanted to earn enough return for boosting their retirement savings. And who would have benefited from this financialization of Social Security? Wall Street fat cats, of course, many of them old friends of Pete Peterson. Millions of Americans suddenly would need to pay consultant fees to figure out how to invest their money, not to mention transaction fees for the purchasing of stocks and mutual funds. The same Wall Street where Peter Peterson had made his billions and Erskine Bowles his multimillions was salivating over that $2.8 trillion stash, anticipating the gold rush that would come their way from the privatization of Social Security.

Fortunately, the American people were buying none of it. To their credit, many Democrats rallied to defend America's retirement pension system against privatization—even many of the Social Security critics within their party were not willing to go that far. Key Democratic leaders mobilized the public against Bush's attack. Bush's "ownership on your own society" was defeated. But that was not the end of the rhetorical attack, and many political leaders today on both sides of the aisle continue to propose different types of Social Security "reforms" in order to "save" it.[35]

Among those politicians, unfortunately, has been President Barack Obama. His National Commission on Fiscal Responsibility and Reform has adopted the anti-entitlement language and the Peterson-led posture of lumping together Social Security with Medicare and Medicaid. As Altman and Kingson point out, we can see how attitudes among the political elite have changed between the Greenspan Commission in 1981 and the Simpson-Bowles Commission in 2010.[36] President Reagan's executive order establishing his commission kept its mission narrowly focused on assuring the financial integrity of Social Security, with no attention on deficits or debt. But President Obama's executive order outlined the goal as that of coming up with recommendations to "balance the budget" and "meaningfully improve the long-run fiscal outlook, including changes to address the growth of entitlement spending and the gap between the projected revenues and expenditures of the Federal Government."[37] Obama's order was expansive, covering all of the federal government's expenditures and lumping together Social Security, Medicare, and Medicaid into what was made to sound like a gigantic federal slush fund for undeserving people. Obama cast aside the narrowly constrained approach deployed so successfully by President Reagan's Greenspan Commission, much to the alarm of the Democratic rank and file, as well as millions of supporters who had voted for him.

Consequently, Obama's Simpson-Bowles Commission accomplished nothing. Yet when compared to the Greenspan Commission, the language and posturing of Obama's cochairs showed how much Pete Peterson and the Goldwater Republicans' ideological battle against Social Security, which had been decades in the making, had gained significant ground. Without the party of FDR to defend it—and unfortunately, the Democrats are no longer that—the New Deal had been severely weakened. Bipartisan consensus over entitlements had been achieved by rolling back the most progressive legislative achievements of the twentieth century. With leaders in both parties devising plans to cut back and in some cases even chop off the only remaining solid leg of the three-legged stool of retirement security, the only obstacle preventing them from this folly has been the American people.

The Architecture of Deform

How did the party of FDR reach this state of abasement? Mike Lofgren, a former high-powered Republican congressional staffer who served for nearly three decades as a chief analyst for both the House and Senate budget committees, provides an eyewitness account of watching the Democrats cede the battlefield to Republicans. In his book *The Party Is Over: How Republicans Went Crazy, Democrats Became Useless, and the Middle Class Got Shafted*, Lofgren provides an insider's view to the Democratic Party's capitulation.

"You know that Social Security and Medicare are in jeopardy when even Democrats refer to them as entitlements," Lofgren writes. "'Entitlement' has a negative sound in colloquial English: somebody who is 'entitled' selfishly claims something he doesn't really deserve." Why not call them "earned benefits," Lofgren asks, which is what they are because we all contribute payroll taxes to fund them?[38] Or, I wonder, why not call them social insurance as other countries do, emphasizing the "insurance" aspect, which Social Security and Medicare benefits clearly are (since virtually all recipients have had to pay premiums over the course of their lifetimes in order to receive the benefits). All workers pay 6.2 percent of their wages into Social Security and

1.45 percent for Medicare, while the employer matches those amounts. Indeed, employer contributions are ultimately taken out of the workers' wages as well, since that money goes into paying these premiums instead of higher salaries. So this is hardly a welfare handout, as the opponents of Social Security tried to brand it. This *is* insurance, and every one of us pays the premiums; we have *earned* it. It's so simple, yet that explanation never occurs to many politicians.

According to Lofgren, "Republicans don't make that mistake; they are relentlessly on message: it is never the 'estate tax,' it is the 'death tax.'"[39] Democrats have failed to deploy the power of language, symbols, and memes to protect FDR's New Deal legacy, and they are losing the war of words. The Republicans had their language ready, and the Democrats were caught flat-footed when the economic collapse of 2008 struck. Keynesian stimulus was called "socialism," even as the big banks and Wall Street unloaded their debts onto the taxpayer via an emergency government bailout. And then, right on cue, the fiscal hawks began screaming about how the nation was drowning in debt, and how Social Security and Medicare were responsible.

It was a gigantic scam, because any cuts in Americans' earned benefits would only go to pay for the rescue of the banks and their bad loans. In effect, we had socialized the losses and privatized the gains. Which only caused government to look even more inept and corrupt, alienating more people and causing them to turn even more toward a party that wants to further reduce the size and role of government. It's a classic case of a catch-22: damned if you do, damned if you don't. The up and down roller coaster of winner-take-all policymaking has left many Americans scratching their heads, feeling alienated from their political leadership, and casting around for a new messiah to lead them to the promised land. Often they anoint a "gazillionaire," from Ross Perot to Donald Trump, with deep enough pockets to allegedly not be corrupted by the partisanship, cronyism, and bumper-sticker politics in the drive to win elections. How nutty, when our only hope seems to be a wealthy person who has so much money that he or she can't be corrupted by . . . money?

Into this noisy, polarized confusion entered the Tea Party and Trump, the latest populist outpourings of "We the People versus Washington, DC." What does the Democratic Party of today offer these people?

"Essentially nothing," Lofgren says. Despite the fact that Lofgren hails from a conservative party, one can't help but conclude that he is correct. "During the past ten years, I have observed that Democrats are actually growing afraid of Republicans," Lofgren says.[40] They are afraid to contest the battlefield and gun shy about engaging over principles and values. The Democrats' surrender has been so complete that incompetence doesn't seem like a plausible explanation; it seems like willful and deliberate opportunism. This is not the party of FDR, JFK, or LBJ anymore. The center has shifted to the right.

Progressive organizations, leaders, and activists have become deeply unsettled about the Democrats' drift. Roger Hickey, director of the progressive-leaning Campaign for America's Future, characterizes the coming battle over reforming the nation's safety-net programs as a seminal moment for Democrats. "It's a real point of conflict and battle within the Democratic Party. It endangers the Democrats' ability to win elections," he explains. You don't want to go into any election, he adds, with a message of "I'm going to cut Social Security and Medicare benefits." According to Adam Green, cofounder of the Progressive Change Campaign Committee, which is leading a charge for expansion of Social Security, "Social Security in 2016 could be the Iraq of 2008, meaning a definitive issue that primary voters make decisions based on." And Justin Ruben, a leader of the influential eight-million-member progressive organization MoveOn.org is even more adamant. "Any Democrat who is voting to cut Social Security benefits," he says, "is probably kissing his or her presidential aspirations goodbye."[41]

Progressive Democrats saw some relief during the 2016 Democratic primary race for president when two non-Hillary candidates called for expansion of Social Security. Former Maryland governor Martin O'Malley released a plan to increase Social Security benefits, and US senator Bernie Sanders from Vermont called for an expansion of the program and introduced legislation to make Social Security benefits more generous.[42] Sanders proposed to pay for it by eliminating the cap on the payroll tax on all income above $250,000. This way, he said, "millionaires and billionaires pay the same share as everyone else." It was mostly a courageous step, but Sanders's strategy begged the question: Why should those who make $118,500 to $250,000 pay a lower overall rate of Social Security tax than those making less than $118,500? What makes them so special? Is this the "moderately affluent voter" donut-hole exemption for a candidate's political expediency?

Yet Hillary Clinton was the front-runner, head and shoulders above everyone in the small Democratic pack of candidates, and her views remained disturbingly opportunistic. Other key Democratic leaders have continued to bail water for Peter G. Peterson and his agenda. The presidential election in 2016 might be the point in the war where the cannon fire crosses.

Winner Takes Nothing

Clearly Lofgren has a point about the Democrats losing a partisan battle of words and ceding too much political ground. But I find his explanation about why the party of the New Deal has three flat tires to be too simplistic. He tells the "how" and the "when" of the Democratic capitulation, and sheds light on what that has looked like. But he never really helps us understand "why"—*why* would Democrats cede this ground? Political parties are nothing if not vote-maximizing machines, so it must have something to do with the drive to win elections. Do Democratic leaders really feel that Social Security is a losing issue? But with Social Security polling spectacularly well across the political spectrum, how could supporting cuts to Social Security be in the Democrats' interest? Or flipping that, how could defending Social Security by calling for its expansion *not* be a winning issue?

To answer that question, we have to understand the peculiar defects of our eighteenth-century-based political system and its gaming dynamics that have reduced politics to a winner-take-all tug-of-war in which the real losers are the American people.

In a very real sense, elections are a game. I don't mean that in a pejorative sense, I mean "game" as in a board game, like Monopoly or Risk. There are rules about how the game is played and how to win. The antiquated rules of the winner-take-all game, which are the foundation of the US political system, perversely affect an issue like Social Security.

Unfortunately, these winner-take-all rules oftentimes prevent the "will of the majority" from prevailing. The fact is, our electoral process of electing our representatives from one electoral district at a time is carving our nation into red and blue one-party fiefdoms. The Democrats control the cities, most of the coasts, and sizable chunks of the Midwest, while the GOP dominates rural areas and most of the flyover zones between the coasts. Note that this landscape is not simply the result of partisan gerrymandering during the redistricting process, which is the typical explanation for many observers about the lack of political competition. No, this is something different, in which partisan residential patterns—where people live—are outstripping the ability of the mapmakers to greatly affect the outcome of most elections. Each legislative district, whether at federal or state levels, has been branded either Republican red or Democratic blue long before the partisan line drawers sit down at their computers, purely because of where people live. For example, Republican candidates can't normally win a House seat in San Francisco, Los Angeles, or New York City because there are simply too many Democrats living there; similarly, Democrats can't usually win a House seat in solidly red conservative districts in states like Mississippi, Oklahoma, or Alabama. Given the regional partisan demographics, in 90 percent of legislative districts at federal and state levels, it's only possible for one side to win; there are too many of one type of partisan voter packed into that district.[43] Certainly, in a handful of states, partisan gerrymandering has had some well-publicized effects, but in most states it has been a minimal factor.

And in presidential and US Senate elections, such lopsided partisan demographics have made it so that there are fewer than a dozen battleground states. GOP candidates have a hard time winning at the state level in California, New York, and other blue states, and Democratic candidates rarely win a statewide office in Alaska, Tennessee, Mississippi, and many other red states. The nation has balkanized along regional lines, with heavy partisan overtones. This demographic destiny has huge consequences for our politics.

In the handful of competitive House districts or presidential states, the parties circle each other as they try to attract support from key swing voters and simultaneously try to mobilize their electoral base. In the era of the "permanent campaign," each side uses relentless polling and focus groups to figure out the campaign messages used to target these swing voters who decide close elections. Politics collapses into a silly game of sound bites and bumper sticker slogans in what I call the "swing voter serenade." Many of the swing voters live in suburban, ex-urban and rural districts that tend to lean a bit conservative, particularly fiscally, on issues like taxes, big government, spending—and entitlements and Social Security. Entitlements are a two-headed Hydra for these swing voters—one head regards entitlements as "big government programs" for "those people," meaning people not like them, which, for the dominant demographic of white voters, often translates into racial minorities. The other head sees not "entitlements" but programs that help grandmas and grandpas. Many undecided voters in the swing districts and states suffered during the economic crisis that began in 2008, and they are very susceptible to demagoguery and populism (enter the Tea Party).

The task of attracting these undecided, swing voters is of paramount importance if you want to win, whether key legislative districts or statewide races, or the electoral college vote for president in a handful of swing states. As the Democrats have become a more urban-based political party, they are increasingly seen by many swing voters as a party beholden to racial minorities and liberal "big government" spenders. That makes it harder for Democrats to win in these sorts of battleground races, so they contort themselves into all sorts of policy backflips in order to move the party to the center so they can compete.

Unfortunately, the soundness of national policy gets caught in this crossfire. The "swing voter serenade" ensures that even the best politicians pitch their electoral prospects toward a handful of these undecided voters in a handful of battleground districts and states. That distorted atmosphere severely undercuts attempts to pursue sound national policy when it comes to Social Security and entitlements, as well as a host of other issues. These swing voters are what all the polls, focus groups, and fuss are all about. Successful politicians and their clever consultants and strategists are obsessed with discovering the right sound bites and carefully crafted campaign themes to target these key demographics of swing voters. They come up with loaded terms like "entitlements" and "debt" and charge them full of hidden, explosive meaning. They call themselves things like "compassionate conservative" and "New Democrat," when most of their targeted policies are anything but compassionate or new.

Indeed, when George W. Bush was campaigning for president in 2000 against Al Gore, Bush sometimes sounded like a liberal Democrat. He pledged to "save Social Security and Medicare," programs that most Republicans had previously condemned as creeping socialism. At one Michigan rally, "compassionate conservative" Bush took a half step away from Ronald Reagan—who had boldly declared that "government *is* the problem"—when he declared, "We're a nation that says that when somebody can't help themselves, we will as a government."[44] James Dao, writing for the *New York Times*, suggested that "over the course of his campaign, Mr. Bush created a new Republican synthesis; he ran against [retiring president] Bill Clinton and sounded like him at the same time."[45]

And yet once Candidate Bush became President Bush, his effort to save Social Security turned into an ideological sandbagging as he tried to privatize the national pension system. Bush and his advisors like Karl Rove had wagered that during the presidential campaign he could hide his hard-right conservative agenda behind a Reaganesque sunny smile and sound bites like "compassionate conservative." His strategy worked, and he was elected president in an extremely close and controversial election.

Since that time, other politicians and their political consultants have followed a similar playbook. The *Washington Post* reported that during the 2014 congressional elections, when Republicans were in striking distance of winning control of the US Senate, many of their candidates suddenly reversed course and spoke out *against* the idea of trimming Social Security benefits.[46] They pulled a George W. Bush, led by none other than Bush's old chief strategist Rove, who ran ads in several key Senate races that accused the Democratic candidates of supporting a "controversial plan" that "raises the retirement age." The Republican candidates were releasing ads promising to protect Social Security, and—almost comical in their perfidy—citing Democrats' support for the recommendations from Simpson and Bowles, the cochairs of Obama's entitlement commission, as the basis of their charges on Social Security. Simpson was asked to condemn his party's tactic of harshly criticizing Democrats who had supported his own recommendations, but he refused. When it comes to elections, he said, "it's savagery out there." Former Republican senator Judd Gregg of New Hampshire, an original member of the Simpson-Bowles commission and chair of the Pete Peterson–funded group Fix the Debt, concurred, saying, "In elections, you do whatever you think will work."[47]

But certainly President Obama and many Democrats also have shown themselves to be extremely adept at saying different things to different audiences. How many of Obama's nearly 70 million voters in 2008, who heard him defend Social Security during the campaign, would have guessed that, once elected, he would appoint a commission cochaired by committed entitlement slashers? So in our winner-take-all political system, a sizable schism has opened between what candidates *say* they will do to attract swing voters, and what they *actually* do once in office. The Democratic and Republican parties today, their leaders, candidates, and their mad-scientist consultants, use modern campaign techniques like polling and focus groups to figure out the sound bites and the contrived images of the permanent campaign. The dazzling effect results in what has been called "crafted talk" and "simulated responsiveness" used to dupe voters.[48]

Yet in a binary, two-choice system, as a result of the incentives of our winner-take-all elections, voters have very few options when it comes to "tossing the bums out." As we have seen, most districts and states are one-party strongholds, with no competition at all during elections at federal or state levels. Consequently, a deformed, alienating brand of politics has emerged, further confusing an already disengaged and disgusted voting public that has nowhere else to go but to the sidelines. But as more and more voters abandon the field, the game is increasingly left to the partisans who wage their battles using the politics of polarization and division, which then fuels a new round of voter alienation and withdrawal, which in turn cedes even more influence to the partisans. It's a vicious downward cycle, and American politics is mired in its quicksand.

So there is a reason why Democrats have ceded the Social Security battleground to the Republicans, and it's a lot more complicated than Mike Lofgren's explanation that Democrats simply choose the wrong words, or because of inequities in privately financed political campaigns. The Democrats have been whipsawed by the defective architecture of our political system. Privately financed elections are bad enough, but the Republicans are better at playing this winner-take-all game: better at slicing and dicing the electorate into bite-size groupings that can be targeted for manipulative sound bites, better at appealing to demographics of swing voters in key swing districts and states, and better at knowing how to position its candidates in the mayhem of political campaigns. Once in government, the more inept the GOP can make government look, the more voters want a party in power that promises them less government. It's a sinister game, what I call the "mad science" of politics, and the Republicans are masters at playing it.

This zero-sum "if I win, you lose" contest is played out on many political fronts, but nowhere has it been more impactful—and potentially more tragic—than in the battle over entitlements and Social Security. Why would older and mostly white Americans who are so dependent on Social Security and Medicare pull the lever for candidates who want to "reform entitlements" (i.e., privatize Social Security and voucherize Medicare) and pass other policies that seem directly counter to their economic self-interest?

Thomas Frank puzzled over this phenomenon in his book *What's the Matter with Kansas?*, locating the source of the tension in the culture wars that trumped politics. Certainly that plays a role, but Frank and many other commentators have overlooked the role that the architecture of our winner-take-all political system itself plays in this dynamic. Polls tell us that most of these voters support Social Security and Medicare, but their vote isn't decided by that issue, particularly since not even the Democrats will lead with it and make it a front-burner campaign theme. Instead, Democrats cede the "entitlement battlefield," allowing GOP strategists to expertly target the swing voters in swing races with wedge issues like guns, gays, babies, immigration, crime, and race. Tragically, on the key issue of Social Security and other safety net supports, there is little obvious difference during high-profile campaigns between the major parties. Given the coziness of a two-choice system in which 90 percent of legislative races and battleground states are lopsidedly safe for one party or the other, both parties throw themselves at the swing voters, who usually have other things on their minds than Social Security or Medicare.

Consequently, although three-quarters of Americans depend heavily on Social Security in their elderly years, the popular program has become a political football. Our nation's politics, cemented into our winner-take-all political system, is taking us in the exact opposite direction that we need to go.

Cracks of Dissent Within the Establishment

Fortunately there are a few leaders trying to yank back hard and pull this tug-of-war in another direction. These include Senators Elizabeth Warren, Tom Harkin, Marck Begich, Jeff Merkley, Sherrod Brown, and Bernie Sanders, and Representatives Keith Ellison, Peter DeFazio, John Larson, Ted Deutch, and John Conyers, all Democrats. Some conservative leaders like Donald Trump, and organizations like the Tea Party, don't always follow the GOP establishment's line on cutting or privatizing Social Security. Despite holding many other traditional conservative views, Trump has been a strong defender of Social Security and

Medicare, an Eisenhower Republican in that way. Many Republicans, he says, believe "Social Security and Medicare are wasteful 'entitlement programs.' But people who think this way need to rethink their position. It's not unreasonable for people who paid into a system for decades to expect to get their money's worth—that's not an 'entitlement'; that's honoring a deal." Similarly on Medicare, Trump argues, "People have lived up to their end of the bargain and paid into the program in good faith. Of course they believe they're 'entitled' to receive the benefits they paid for—they are!"[49]

It is the height of irony—and a reflection of the strange odyssey of the Democratic Party—that the bombastic Trump has been a more staunch supporter of safeguarding entitlement programs for retirees than either President Obama or Bill or Hillary Clinton. And he has taken on the conservative establishment, including the other GOP presidential candidates in the 2016 election, giving voice to the nearly 7 out of 10 rank-and-file Republicans who support Social Security. He hasn't gone so far, however, as to call for an expansion of Social Security. But with Democratic senators Warren and Sanders leading the way, 43 out of 100 US senators and 116 out of 435 US House members have gone on record in favor of expansion, as have leading progressive economists like Paul Krugman and Dean Baker.[50]

Both the Democratic and Republican establishments have reneged on their commitment to everyday Americans. Both political parties are selling out on many important bread-and-butter fronts, including the highly popular Social Security. With US elections bedeviled by winner-take-all games and private campaign donations, both parties have become the parties of narrow special interests, marinated in money, and run by what Mike Lofgren and others have called a "deep state" of shadowy hybrid alliances of government with top finance, national security, and private industry honchos. These elite and powerful interests have been able to undermine government itself, and to pursue their agenda with only a genuflection toward democratic accountability.[51]

All of this may be building to a boil. Social Security remains one of the key issues of our times, both in terms of its symbolic importance as well as its policy impact. It could yet become a crucial wedge issue that the politicians dance around in their swing-voter serenade to attract voters and win elections. With polls consistently showing that a wide political swathe of everyday Americans strongly supports Social Security, how long can this corruption of politics continue to hold back the popular will?

CHAPTER FOUR

The Nine Biggest Myths and Lies about Social Security

Social Security is bankrupting us. It's outdated. It's a Ponzi scheme. It's socialism. It's stealing from young people. The opponents and pundits determined to roll back the United States to the "good old days" before the New Deal regularly trot out a number of bogeymen and bigfoots to scare Americans into not supporting their own retirement well-being. That hasn't worked too well. Americans of all political stripes remain strongly supportive of Social Security and other so-called "entitlements" like Medicare. But the other reason for plastering the media waves with a chorus of myths and lies is to stir up a political climate in Washington, DC, that causes politicians of both parties to cease looking for better alternatives other than to cut, cut, cut, or even to maintain the inadequate status quo. Below are rebuttals to some of the biggest whoppers regularly told about one of the most popular and successful federal programs in our nation's history.

1. Social Security is going broke and will bankrupt the country.

Social Security is not going broke, not by a long shot. The Social Security Board of Trustees released its annual report to Congress in July 2015, and among all the tables, charts, and graphs in that big fat report, it would be easy to miss the most important take-home message: Social Security is one of the best-funded federal programs in US history. That's because it has its own dedicated revenue stream, which is composed of the insurance premiums paid by every worker (deducted from our paychecks by what is called "payroll contributions"), which are automatically banked into the Trust Fund.[1] Even the Pentagon and the defense budget do not have their own dedicated revenue stream.

In fact, Social Security has not one dedicated revenue stream, but *three*. Besides the payroll contributions, Social Security is also funded by income generated from investing all those set-aside wages into US treasuries. That money earns a sizable return on the investment. And Social Security is also funded by revenue that comes from levying income tax on Social Security recipients (yes, your Social Security check and that of other Americans is treated as income and taxed—and it brought in $756 billion to the Trust Fund in 2014). Those three revenue streams combined have banked $2.8 *trillion* in the Trust Fund and resulted in a $25 billion *surplus* in 2014.

Bankrupt? That charge does not even pass a good laugh test.

Indeed, because Social Security has its own funding source, and by law is not allowed to spend any money it does not have, it is actually impossible for Social Security to add to annual operating deficits or the national debt. Moreover, the Social Security Board of Trustees is required by law to report to Congress every year about the financial fitness of the program. The annual trustees report projects its revenues and payouts, not just for the next five, ten, or twenty years, but for the next seventy-five years. It's one of the few programs anyone can identify that has had the wisdom to plan for the future, rather than planning around short-term political calculations and the next election cycle.

Pensions expert Nancy Altman analyzed the trustees' report in 2015 and concluded, "Over the next 5 years, Social Security has sufficient funds to pay every penny of benefits and every penny of associated administrative costs. That is true for the next 10 years. And also the next 15 years."[2] However over the next twenty years, as more and more of the huge population bloom known as the baby boomers continues to retire, Social Security is projecting a modest shortfall of just 0.51 percent of gross domestic product (GDP). If nothing is done to plug that gap, sometime in the 2030s the Trust Fund will have enough to cover only 75 percent of benefits. But there are so many budgetary ways to cover that shortfall, it becomes clear that the problem is not the finances of finding the money but the politics of partisanship and paralysis. No other government program can claim that it is fully funded for almost the next quarter century. What government critics ever say that the Defense Department or the Departments of Energy or Education are going bankrupt? Yet those programs don't have dedicated revenue streams, and certainly no one plans or projects costs for those programs over the next seventy-five years.

No, these sorts of charges are leveled by the Peter G. Petersons of the world for political reasons, not economics or finances. And even in terms of the shortfall that will emerge in a couple of decades, that gap could be covered with a few minor tweaks. For example, simply removing the payroll cap and taxing all income brackets equally would not only be fairer to all Americans, it would also raise all of the money and then some to plug any Social Security funding shortfalls twenty years from now. So we would have lots of time to phase in a fair reform like that. Opinion polls have demonstrated that most Americans think if they pay Social Security tax on their full salary, others should as well. So removing the income cap and making all income levels pay according to the same rules would be a very popular reform, and would safeguard the nearly $3 trillion Trust Fund for decades to come. That's just one example of the many adjustments we can enact that would make the US retirement system more fair, robust, and stable, and better adapted to the realities of today's economy. (In the next chapter, I will explore other funding options that will not only stabilize Social Security, but will double its monthly payout.)

2. Social Security is unsustainable because we have fewer workers for every retiree, even as our society is "greying" and people are living longer.

Another charge leveled by critics is that the number of workers compared to the number of non-workers—what is known as the dependency ratio—is declining, and so as a result Social Security is unsustainable. President George W. Bush really pushed hard on this point in his bid to gut the program and turn it into private accounts. In his 2005 State of the Union address, President Bush said:

> Social Security was created decades ago, for a very different era. . . . A half-century ago, about 16 workers paid into the system for each person drawing benefits. . . . Instead of 16 workers paying in for every beneficiary, right now it's only about three workers. And over the next few decades, that number will fall to just two workers per beneficiary. . . . With each passing year, fewer workers are paying ever-higher benefits to an ever-larger number of retirees.[3]

President Bush's key strategist, Karl Rove, had the president tour the country to promote his privatization plan for Social Security, and he repeated his talking points everywhere he went, in state after state and city after city. President Bush must have set some kind of record: rarely has anyone been so wrong so often about Social Security as the president was during his "privatization or bust" tour.

Yet this claim by not only President Bush but key Republican and even some Democratic leaders reflects a deep misunderstanding. The fact is, the 16 to 1 ratio comes from the initial years of Social Security when it was dramatically ramped up to cover millions of new workers. Because these new workers were still employed and contributing their premiums through payroll contributions into Social Security, none of them were as yet collecting any benefits. So initially there were not that many beneficiaries, compared to the number of workers paying into the program. As Nancy Altman and Eric Kingson point out in *Social Security Works!*, "This is the kind of ratio experienced by all pension plans, public and private, at the start when few workers have yet qualified for benefits."[4] By 1955, the worker-to-beneficiary ratio had already been cut in half to around 8 to 1, and by 1975 it was down to 3 to 1. It has remained there for approximately forty years.

And that's just a small slice of the overall picture. The "dependency ratio" is not just a factor of the number of workers compared to the number of retirees. It has to be configured according to the number of total dependents, including children. A different picture emerges when children are included.

The fact is, declining birthrates have resulted in a fall in dependent children, so the rise in the number of retired will be partly offset by a decline in the number of dependent children. According to Gary Burtless, an economist and demographic expert at the Brookings Institution, when the decline in children is factored in, total dependency ratios in many countries in 2050 will look more favorable than the ratios were in the 1960s, when the majority of the baby boom generation were still children. In the United States, for example, the dependency ratio peaked in 1965, when there were ninety-five dependents (both children and retirees) for every one hundred working adults. By 2050 the figure will be eighty dependents for every hundred workers, which, while much higher than the highly favorable figure of forty-nine dependents in 2000, will still be markedly lower than the number of dependents in 1965. "The crisis of supporting a large future dependent population will evidently involve a smaller burden than was borne by working age adults in the 1960s," Burtless says.[5]

How did we as a society manage to get wealthier in the 1960s and '70s despite such a much higher dependency ratio? The answer, in a word, is "productivity." Labor productivity is a measure of the amount of goods and services produced by each worker, which in a well-functioning economy increases over time due to the implementation of technology, greater education and job skills training, as well as more efficient business practices. If our labor productivity continues to increase, and the political system passes on the economic gains in the form of a broadly shared prosperity, then the rising tide will float all boats. Political analyst Michael Lind has argued that "productivity growth can solve much or all of the pension funding problem," and as proof of that he points out that if the ratio of workers to retirees goes from 3 to 1 today to the expected 2 to 1 in the future, that is quite a minor shift compared to a change from a ratio of 16 workers to 1 retiree in 1950, or even 8 workers to 1 in 1960, to 3 to 1 today—a shift made relatively smooth and painless by education, training, and technology-driven productivity growth over the past half century.

Gary Burtless agrees, saying that the measure of dependency "does not provide a meaningful measure of worker welfare. Workers are presumably much more concerned with the actual consumption they can afford," rather than the amount they have to pay out of their wages for all dependents. "If real wages . . . rise fast enough, future workers who face a higher dependency burden can enjoy higher levels of real consumption than present-day workers who face a smaller dependency burden." If wages and incomes continue to rise as fast as they have during the past sixty years, Burtless explains, future workers will enjoy higher consumption than today's workers *in spite of* a ratio of fewer workers per dependents. That's because "an overwhelming share of the growth in final consumption is due to higher worker productivity. . . . The growth in output per worker has been fast enough so that it has overwhelmed the impact of a higher dependency burden, and this is likely to remain true in the future."[6]

That's academic-ese for saying another Social Security myth bites the dust. That doesn't mean that we can ignore factors like dependency ratios, but the fact is that as long as our economy is healthy, robust, and growing, creating jobs and increasing productivity, and the political system is inclusive and passes on the increased prosperity to the general public in the form of higher wages and a robust safety net, there is no reason that the greying of society or the ratio of workers to dependents should hamper the nation's economic future.

3. **IRAs and 401(k)s have replaced private pensions and Social Security. Americans want to be self-reliant on their own private retirement accounts, because you can do better investing on your own.**
One would think that the volatility and havoc wreaked by the stock market in recent years would have laid to rest the notion that "self-reliant" Americans can invest and save on their own. It's really not that easy to build up a private nest egg sufficient for the nearly $1 million in savings that an individual will need to cover their needs during their postwork years. As noted in chapter 1, the fact that three-quarters of Americans nearing retirement age have less than $30,000 in their private savings—less than 5 percent of what they will need—shows what a bust of an idea this really is.

For years, advocates for deregulation and entitlements have pushed for privatized retirement accounts—401(k)s, IRAs, and other private savings vehicles managed by Wall Street's financial managers, which skims off the top their own lucrative fees. At the same time, businesses have pushed to shut down their "defined-benefit" pensions, which have long provided a guaranteed monthly payout for life, just like Social Security's lifetime annuity. Now that we have nearly three decades of experience with replacing pensions with 401(k)s and IRAs, and of Americans trying so hard to stuff their retirement piñatas, it's clear that most American retirees are no more secure than before. In fact, they are much less secure.

The 401(k) system that was positioned in the 1980s to replace pensions was sold to American workers as the new and improved successors to the guaranteed payout of a defined-benefit pension. Business leaders and the politicians took away what worked and replaced it with an experiment. But that experiment has failed, and proven to be more fragile and inefficient than the system it replaced. Besides having failed to produce enough retirement savings for the vast majority of Americans, the 401(k) system has forced everyday Americans to face a number of significant risks. The most obvious of these risks is that you can lose your personal savings to unpredictable stock market gyrations or a housing-market downturn, especially since most people have little expertise in how to navigate the ups and downs. But there is also the uncomfortable fact that, with wages flat over the last few decades, millions of individual workers have been unable to save enough. Consequently, as we have seen, 80 percent of the federal subsidy for individual retirement savings goes to the top 20 percent of income earners—the people who need it the least.

For all of these reasons, the transition to this individualized and privatized system has not turned out to be the pot of gold at the end of the retirement rainbow that was originally promised. Indeed, about a third of households don't have a savings account at all, let alone savings. And according to a Federal Reserve study, as discussed in chapter 2, nearly half of all households don't have the savings to deal with an unexpected expense of a mere $400.[7] Indeed, in a vicious cycle, the need for "survival money" is so great that many workers have been forced to tap into their 401(k)s early, before retirement, which carries heavy penalties. In 2010, following the 2008 collapse, contributions to defined-contribution pensions totaled $176 billion, while early withdrawals totaled $60 billion. These are not the hallmarks of a successful retirement system.

And let's be clear: most businesses claimed they were eliminating their company pensions and replacing them with a 401(k)-type savings plan as a cost-saving measure—yet those same companies paid increasingly astronomical salaries and bonus packages to their executives. There's no question that US workers were insured more efficiently and more securely under the traditional company pension system which provided a guaranteed monthly payout for the rest of the retiree's life. Various reforms that have been proposed to 401(k)s and IRAs would not repair this fundamentally broken system of private savings vehicles. They have manifestly failed to stabilize the retirement system in the aftermath of the collapse of private company pensions and personal savings. After three decades, it's time to admit this experiment has failed.

Another way to think of Social Security is as a form of "wage insurance." Just as we have health insurance, car insurance, and home insurance, we need insurance for when we are too old to earn wages anymore. That's what Social Security is, when you get right down to it: insurance against your loss of wages during your elderly years. You pay into it all of your working life; it's not asking too much for it to provide you with a comfortably secure safety net in your post-working life.

4. **Social Security is stealing from young people and saddling them with a level of overwhelming debt.**
Billionaire Peter G. Peterson has been one of the pioneers of this kind of intergenerational doomsaying. Headlines about the old stealing from the young certainly grab the media spotlight. But this one is an old, old trope that never made any sense. Peterson first raised it back in 1982, in the midst of the deliberations of the Greenspan Commission. Social Security, Peterson wrote, "threatens the entire economy. . . . The Social Security system will run huge deficits . . . these deficits will push our children into a situation of economic stagnation and social conflict and create a potentially disastrous situation for the elderly of the future."[8]

Peterson became greatly distressed when the Greenspan Commission did not undertake his prescribed overhaul of Social Security. So after Peterson made his billions on Wall Street, he founded his eponymous Peterson Foundation, as well as other organizations like the Concord Coalition and Committee for a Responsible Federal Budget, to help promote his wild-eyed prophecies about the coming intergenerational war. He has used his various organizations to, among other crusades, fund college and high school campaigns and organizations called "Up to Us," The Can Kicks Back, Lead . . . or Leave, and Third Millennium, which have served as the youth arm of his various entitlement-busting efforts. The Can Kicks

Back president Ryan Schoenike was quoted in the *Washington Post* as saying, "The [federal] debt is now the top of line issue for most young people," but *Salon*'s Alex Pareene called that "a weird lie." Pareene also pointed out that this wasn't the first "pretend youth group" founded or funded by Peterson.[9] Peterson has spent a good chunk of his billions stirring up a youthful mob with pitchforks, pushing them to bang at the gates of their grandmas and grandpas for stealing their birthright.

But Peterson hasn't been the only Cassandra prophesying a generational war between young and old. More recently, the *Washington Post*'s Robert J. Samuelson took up the cause. "We need to stop coddling the elderly," he wrote in a 2013 column, calling Social Security and Medicare "a growing transfer from the young, who are increasingly disadvantaged, to the elderly, who are increasingly advantaged."[10] In a 2014 column, Samuelson continued his anti-elderly and antigovernment debt diatribe, writing, "Giving the elderly as a class special treatment heaps the costs of deficit reduction on workers and children."[11]

Pitting the elderly against children makes little sense for many reasons, but one obvious one is that today's children will one day be seniors themselves. And they will need the retirement benefits that people like Peterson and Samuelson are trying to cut from retirees. Robbing Peter to pay Paul might make sense from a maniacally focused budget buster's perspective, but it makes little sense from a public policy perspective. If that makes sense, then why not cut funding from cancer research, or diabetes treatment, since those ailments mostly affect older people and not the young. But obviously the young today could be attacked by those ailments tomorrow. Society benefits as a whole when it tries to address conditions that affect humanity as a whole.

One of those conditions is growing old. Everyone will pass through that stage of life (unless death comes knocking prematurely), and it makes no sense to not do all that is humanely and financially possible to help the elderly. Otherwise, where might this sort of knee-jerk reaction end? Why not pit middle-aged people and their needs against seniors?

Or against children, for that matter? Or, as Altman and Kingson put it, "There is much more inequality within any given age group than there is between age groups."[12] For example, there is a lot more inequality between wealthy seniors and poor seniors, and between youth from wealthy and poor families, than there is between seniors and youngsters. It simply makes no sense to carve up the class distinctions in this way and point an incriminating finger that pits the young against the old.

Interestingly, economist Dean Baker, from the Center for Economic Policy and Research, points out that other countries have successfully supported *both* the elderly and the young. According to Baker, "Countries that spend a larger share of their GDP supporting their seniors also spend a larger share of their income supporting the young." In his study, Baker found that a dollar of additional per capita spending on kids is associated with sixty-seven cents of additional spending on seniors. In other words, he says, it's not a case of one or the other. "The countries that are willing to spend more to support their seniors are also willing to spend more to ensure that their kids get a decent start in life."[13] And in looking at policy choices over the past couple of decades, what becomes additionally clear is that any savings from cuts to Social Security and Medicare are not necessarily going to benefit programs for children. More likely they will end up as tax cuts for businesses, banks, or the wealthy, or will pay for the latest high-tech versions of military equipment.

In fact, if you want to really deal with the sources of debt that will drown the prospects of younger people, let's talk about health-care costs. The nation now spends over 17 percent of our GDP on health care, which is twice as much as the amount spent by virtually every other developed nation (and we only cover about 89 percent of the US population, compared to those nations covering 100 percent). Those costs are simply unsustainable and will bankrupt future generations. Note that cutting Medicare or Medicaid benefits, as the Pete Peterson's of the world want to do, will solve nothing because it will just push those costs onto the private sector (in fact, that would make things even worse, since Medicare and Medicaid are actually much more cost efficient than the private health-care system). So yes, future generations will in fact drown in debt—if we don't address health-care-cost inflation. But that has nothing to do with Social Security, or even the thrifty Medicare.

Social Security will always have somewhat of a perception problem among younger Americans. For a certain number, it will always be viewed as "money for old people who get it from the government." For people of any age who are working and having taxes deducted from their paychecks, Social Security is a benefit for someone else—elderly retirees. But at some point in their life, those people will no longer be able to work, and, like any type of insurance, Social Security will be there to protect them with "wage insurance" from a complete loss of earned income. Social Security is *self-insurance* in that way, that is, protection against the risks we all face due to old age, disability, or death. That's a point that must be brought home to every new generation of young Americans.

And the evidence shows that younger people are figuring it out. Much to the chagrin of the "generational war" propagandists, their campaign does not seem to be gaining traction. A poll in August 2015 commissioned by senior advocacy group AARP found that nine in ten young people (adults under thirty) believe Social Security is an important government program, and nearly nine in ten (85 percent) want to know it will be there when they retire.[14] Nevertheless, the fact that this baseless idea periodically arises from the crypt is proof that if enough money is thrown at a bad notion, it can live forever.

5. We have to raise the retirement age because people are living longer and the nation can't afford to pay for all these aging retirees.

Wrong. We do not have to raise the retirement age. As we will see in the next chapter, there are common-sense changes we can make to Social Security that would not only safeguard it financially for the future, but would actually allow us to *double* the monthly benefits for retirees. For example, we could increase tax fairness by lifting the cap on the payroll tax so that wealthy Americans make the same percentage contribution as every other American. At the same time, the payroll contribution base could be extended to profits from investment income, such as capital gains. This would raise additional revenues in a progressive fashion that could be used to enhance the program for all Americans.

Also, it's not exactly true that everyone is living longer. Only some of us are. People with higher incomes and more education, especially men, are the ones who have gained the most in life expectancy.[15] There is a myth that Americans tend to stop working in their early sixties, shortly after becoming eligible for (reduced) Social Security benefits at age sixty-two and well before the designated "full" retirement age of sixty-six, but in fact that's not the case. Studies of the labor force participation rate of US workers show that the number of older Americans working is high by historical standards, and close to the postwar peak. It's another myth that all these Americans are retiring early.[16]

So raising the retirement age doesn't really solve "the problem" of people retiring too early or living too long. Beyond that, let's be clear—raising the retirement age is the equivalent of a cut in Social Security. In fact, actuarial experts have estimated that raising the retirement age by a year is mathematically equivalent to cutting the amount of lifetime benefits by 6–7 percent. Already the retirement age has been increased to sixty-six years of age from sixty-five, and is due to rise to sixty-seven beginning in 2027. That will amount to a 13 percent benefit cut for all retirees.[17] Proponents of cuts flippantly say that people can make up the shortfall by working longer. But that mentality doesn't even consider the fact that as people age, it becomes harder and harder to find or retain decent employment. With headlines blaring that robots and automation are taking over our jobs, Americans in their fifties and early sixties who lose their employment are having a harder time getting back into the workforce. So they may have no choice but to retire early at sixty-two and start taking their Social Security benefits. Yet, because of the rules of how Social Security works, it will be at a much reduced benefit level that will stay permanent throughout their retired life.

Now the budget busters are proposing that we increase the retirement age yet again, to seventy years old. We haven't even had a chance to assess the impact of an increase to sixty-seven years on low-income workers, minorities, women, and other vulnerable populations, yet already some are eager to cut retirement benefits further still. One of the foremost proponents of this idea has been Alicia Munnell, an economist and professor at Boston College. Munnell is one of the nation's foremost retirement scholars, who has added immeasurably to our understanding, but on this point, I think she is quite wrong. In a recent book she coauthored, titled *Falling Short: The Coming Retirement Crisis and What to Do About It*, she proposed a "pull yourself up by your bootstraps" solution to the retirement crisis, in essence a proposal that Americans should save more and work longer.

Munnell and her coauthors recommended making 401(k)s mandatory, even though all the research shows that most people do not have enough discretionary income to put into their 401(k), even if they had one. And with interest rates so low, it means these people would need to risk that money in the stock market to get decent returns, despite their lack of expertise in stock market investment. The authors also recommend reverse mortgages for tapping into one's house as a retirement vehicle, which might work fine for those who own a home, but even then, as we saw in the economic collapse of 2008, a home can be a risky investment.[18]

This is not the first time Munnell has proposed these sorts of measures. In 2009, in her coauthored book *Working Longer: The Solution to the Retirement Income Challenge*, she proposed much the same.[19] In short, these sorts of proposals do not really grapple with the extent of the retirement crisis, and Munnell's solutions would likely help only a small number of strongly self-directed individuals with sufficient income that allows them to save. But her recommendation that Social Security benefits should not begin until seventy years old represents a huge cut in Social Security benefits. With each additional year added to the retirement age equaling a 6–7 percent cut in benefits, Munnell's proposal is the equivalent of cutting benefits by a third, when compared to the previous retirement age of sixty-five years, and a 20 percent cut over the future retirement age of sixty-seven. These proposals are taking us backward. There are better ways to pay for Social Security, not only to maintain the status quo but to actually expand it.

6. **Social Security's disability program will run out of money by the end of 2016, and then sometime in the 2030s the retirement portion will also run out.**

Finally, the prophets of doom can say they were right all along. Besides paying retirement benefits to tens of millions of Americans, the Social Security program also has a separate disability program for those 11 million Americans of whatever age who are too disabled to work. Yet these disability recipients face steep benefit cuts by the end of 2016 unless Congress acts. That's because, according to the 2015 Social Security Trustees Report, the disability trust fund will run out of money in the middle of a presidential election year, which would trigger an automatic 19 percent cut in benefits.[20]

Hah, say the budget busters, you see? We told you, first it's going to happen to the disability program, and not long after that it will happen to the retirement program.

That sounds ominous, but in fact it's not correct. By law, the payroll premiums deducted from all workers' paychecks are divided between the disability trust fund and Social Security's much larger retirement fund. The retirement fund is supposed to receive about 85 percent of the money, and the rest goes to disability to provide benefits to Americans with serious and permanent disabilities, as well as to their families.[21]

But over the past twenty years, for various reasons, the fund balances have gotten out of whack, causing a temporary shortfall in the amount allocated to the disability fund. Congress can easily fix this by simply redirecting a small amount of the revenue already in the retirement fund to the disability fund. It has done this several times in the past, most recently in 1994. If Congress were to do this, the retirement fund would lose only one year of solvency, but we would have nearly twenty years to figure out a longer-term solution to any underfunding in the 2030s.

In the past, this has always been a simple fix. But in today's poisoned partisan climate, nothing with the word "Congress" in it is simple. The Republicans, in particular, but also some conservative Democrats, are using this "bankruptcy moment" to score points in their drive to slash away at entitlements. Republicans claim that simply redirecting the revenue would be taking money from retired workers to pay disabled workers— robbing one fund to finance another. They are demanding reductions in disability benefits—which go to the most vulnerable Americans—as well as restrictions on eligibility. They are also insisting on new measures to combat fraud—an old Republican canard for attacking government programs, from welfare to food stamps to voting—though no one has proven that the disability program is rife with fraud.

The GOP budget fire breathers have their work cut out for them in trying to publicize the usual scare stories about "disability queens" cheating the system. Most disability beneficiaries were earning middle incomes when they became disabled, averaging a little more than $42,000 a year. And now, their disability checks? About $14,000 a year.[22] That's less money than a full-time minimum-wage worker earns, to support American workers who have been tragically injured with serious and permanent disabilities. *That* is the type of "waste and fraud" that apparently causes the entitlement slashers to go ballistic.

It's not like the shortage of money in the disability trust fund wasn't predictable. In fact, it was entirely expected. Known demographic factors like the aging of the large cohort of baby boomers has resulted in more people seeking disability benefits. In addition, the increase in the number of women in the labor force has led to more disabled workers and a rise in payments from the fund. The solution should be fairly simple, as it has been in the past—just redirect revenue from the retirement to the disability trust fund. But opponents of entitlements are using their timeworn tactic of manufacturing a crisis and holding disabled Americans as their hostages in their ideological battle to force negotiations over other budget cuts they want. This is another example of the politicians playing winner-take-all sandbox games over important national policy, even with an extremely popular program like Social Security, and even if it's going to hurt the most disadvantaged among us.

7. **Social Security is un-American and too "socialistic" for most people in the United States.**
   Un-American? Too socialist? Social Security remains one of the most popular and successful government programs in history—opinion polls show nearly 70 percent of *Republicans* don't want it to be cut or hurt. So if Social Security is too "socialist," Americans must all be a bunch of closet socialists. Millions of Americans from all political persuasions now depend on Social Security, and no amount of divisive rhetoric, or even Pete Peterson's billions of dollars, can change that fact.

8. **Social Security is old-fashioned and a relic from another era. The Greenspan Commission made cutbacks in 1983, and now we have to cut back further.**
   A brief history of the Social Security program reveals something important: its *expansion* is more in keeping with US tradition and the history of this popular program than its *rollback*. In 1935, eligibility for social security was so limited that only a minority of the population could hope to benefit from social insurance. Entire categories of Americans were excluded, most notably the majority of blacks and women. In addition, huge occupational categories such as maritime, transportation, and agricultural workers were excluded, so

that even the majority of white men were ineligible. Social Security was established as a complementary system to the private retirement system, intended to provide only a basic foundation for private employer pensions to build upon.

Consequently, initial benefits were extremely low by today's standards—the first Social Security benefit, for example, was only about $300 a month in 2008 dollars. In 1937, Social Security had barely 53,000 beneficiaries and they were paid a total of only $1.3 million. But within three years those numbers increased more than fourfold, to 222,000 beneficiaries and $35 million. Still, Social Security was kept on a short leash by an alliance of conservative Republicans and Southern Democrats (known as Dixiecrats) who first blocked and then delayed the expansion of payroll tax rates after 1937, which kept the system underfinanced.[23] The combination of ongoing political opposition, limited revenue, and limited benefits, and a series of decisions on how private pensions would be treated favorably by the Internal Revenue Service, acted as severe constraints on Social Security's initial growth.

But over the next forty years, Social Security was to prove its worth, again and again. It was more efficient, more portable, and slowly became more universal than private pensions. The system was amended repeatedly to expand eligibility, raise the level and variety of benefits, and establish innovative programs to cover new populations. A Trust Fund was established that allowed the system to support a higher benefit level. In 1939 benefits were added for survivors and the retiree's spouse and children. In 1956 disability benefits were added, and agricultural and domestic workers were included, adding the majority of African Americans to both Old Age and Unemployment Insurance programs. In 1965, a related program, Medicare, which provides health insurance for the elderly, was signed into law. In 1972, Social Security benefits became indexed to inflation with a permanent cost-of-living adjustment (COLA); Supplemental Security Income, which provides an additional pension for the elderly poor, was established two years later.[24]

Over this time, as the population increased, participation in Social Security correspondingly increased as well. By 1950 there were 3.5 million beneficiaries who were paid a total of $961 million; by 1960, 14.8 million beneficiaries and $11.2 billion; by 1970, 26 million beneficiaries and $32 billion; nearly 36 million beneficiaries and $121 billion by 1980; and about 40 million beneficiaries and $248 billion by 1990 (all figures unadjusted for inflation).[25] However, as Social Security expanded over the years to include those with disabilities, spouses, and survivors, the number of beneficiaries began to include more Americans who were not elderly retirees. In 2015, about 65 million Americans were receiving Social Security benefits of one kind or another; of that number, about 43 million were retired seniors or their spouses sixty-five years or older, collecting retirement benefits. The cost to provide benefits to just that population of retirees currently amounts to about $662 billion per year.[26]

That's a lot of money. In terms of the amount of dollars, the Social Security program is one of the single largest expenditures in the federal budget, with 20.8 percent of the budget spent on Social Security, compared to 20.1 percent for Medicare/Medicaid and 20.5 percent for the Pentagon's defense budget (though that amount does not include what was spent on the Iraqi and Afghan wars, as well as on other federal agencies involved in defense-related activities, such as the Department of Homeland Security, Department of Energy, Veterans Administration, and others).[27] Social Security is currently the largest social insurance program in the United States, estimated to keep roughly 40 percent of all Americans age sixty-five or older out of poverty.

So the history of Social Security has been more one of expansion than retraction since the 1930s, shifting in response to economic downturns as well as concerns over demographics. It is important to reacquaint the public with that history for the battles that loom ahead. Legislatively speaking, the federal amendment process is the means by which Social Security became the political cornerstone that it is today. This history of gradual expansion through amendment has benefited from the known traditions and customs of Congress. Members of Congress are very familiar with the stakeholders and interest groups aligned on this issue, as well as the ins and outs of the amendment process. Perhaps not coincidentally, researcher Steven Attewell points out that virtually all of the previous Social Security amendments "were passed in the autumn of election years when voters were paying the most attention to Congress."[28] Amending the Social Security Act little by little over time, taking on manageable bite sizes that the political system can cope with, has been the right vehicle for enacting sweeping public policy changes.

Attewell, a Social Security reform advocate, has proposed that if we want to construct a new system of social protection, history suggests that advocates should "restart this process of regular amendments. Amendments could be offered annually or biannually, each one incorporating gradual expansion." This process should continue until the conditions have been created for providing retirement security for all Americans.[29]

9. The United States already has the world's highest living standard, with an overly generous retirement system for seniors. We must be more realistic.

The United States is a very wealthy country, but because of rising inequality, the enjoyment of that wealth has not spread to as many Americans as in previous decades. Economists and social scientists have created new indexes and statistics to measure the success of an economy, and to determine the quality of life beyond the overused measurements of gross domestic product, unemployment rates, economic growth rates, and the like. These indexes have names such as the Index of Economic Well-Being, Weighted Index of Social Development, United Nations' Human Poverty Index, Genuine Progress Indicator, the Ecological Footprint, and Mothers Index (ranking the best and worst places to be a mother and child). The *Economist* magazine, the World Economic Forum, and the European Commission also have developed their own quality-of-life indexes. These various indexes include a number of human values that are ignored in purely economic calculations, such as income inequality, access to health care, life expectancy, poverty levels, crime rate, ecological sustainability, family/social networks, democracy/political participation, and personal security, among others.

The remarkable thing that stands out is that in nearly every index the United States is an outlier, rated at the *bottom* among developed countries, with only a few indexes rating the US in the middle of the pack. None of them rate the United States at the top. Meanwhile, many European countries, as well as Canada, Japan, Australia, and others, occupy the top ratings. Such side-by-side comparisons with other developed countries undermine the credibility of American claims of economic superiority or leadership.

One of the reasons these other nations surpass the United States is because many of them have more robust national retirement systems. They take better care of their elderly people, not only through an adequate individual pension but also with better housing policies, much less expensive health care, more efficient mass transportations systems, and other ways that have reduced the cost of living for seniors.

Indeed, the United States is quite a bit less generous to its retirees than other developed nations. The Organisation for Economic Co-operation and Development (OECD) is an alliance of thirty-four developed countries committed to democracy and a market economy, and it tracks and compares features like national pension systems. According to its numbers, the US pension "replacement rate" for the average earner—the share of gross income the pension is expected to replace—is 38.3 percent, which is below the OECD average of 54.4 percent and 58 percent for countries in the European Union.[30] For low-income workers—defined as earning 50 percent of the average wage—the United States was even more stingy, with a replacement rate of 49.5 percent compared to the OECD average of 71 percent and 73.9 percent for EU countries. Like in the United States, retirement pensions in most of these other nations are funded by regular payroll deductions from both workers and employers.

On other replacement metrics like "transfers in retirement income," which measures the share of retirement income made up by both public pensions and social welfare assistance, the United States also looks stingy. The OECD average is 58.6 percent while the US average is only 37.6 percent, barely half the average of the EU countries at 70.6 percent and just above Mexico and South Korea. Consequently, the poverty rate for seniors in the United States is substantially higher than in most other OECD countries, nearly 20 percent compared to 12.8 percent in the OECD and 8.9 percent among EU countries in the OECD. The US rate is even higher than in Chile and Turkey.[31]

These measurements by definition mostly assess pensions, which use retirement income as a proxy for relative levels of well-being. But that income is used to purchase the services, food, shelter, medical care, and other items that a retiree needs. In many developed nations, health care, transportation/mass transit, senior care in institutions, and other senior services are less expensive and more cost efficient than in the United States. Natixis Global Asset Management, an investment firm that publishes its own annual Global Retirement Index, rates countries based on twenty key trends across four broad categories: health, material well-being, finances, and quality of life. Together, these trends "provide a measure of the life conditions and well-being expected by retirees."

In the 2015 index (see figure 4.1), the US retirement system placed nineteenth globally for the third year in a row, ranked behind nearly every advanced nation except the United Kingdom and Italy. The United States was ranked behind Switzerland, Norway (ranked first and second, respectively), Japan, Germany, France, Sweden, Canada, Australia, New Zealand, Denmark, Belgium, and others. The United States was even ranked behind countries like the Czech Republic and South Korea.[32]

The United States ranked so low in part due to its over-reliance on unstable private savings plans like 401(k)s and IRAs, and its "relatively large gap in income equality." Many European countries were seen as "leading in quality of retirement," benefiting from "strong pension financing and social programs" and "well-developed and growing industrialized economies with strong financial systems and regulations, broad access to healthcare, and substantial public investment in infrastructure and technology." Despite relatively high tax burdens, these countries "rank high in per-capita income levels and low in income inequality."[33]

To be sure, pension systems in European countries have also faced their own challenges, particularly in the aftermath of the global Great Recession. But mostly they have not experienced the kinds of shocks that private retirement accounts in the United States have endured in the years since the economic collapse. Some European countries like Germany and Greece enacted reforms to their public pension systems, in some cases decreasing what were once extremely generous

Figure 4.1 Natixis Global Retirement Index 2015, Annual Study: The Top 20 Nations (Along with Their Standing in 2014)

1 Switzerland (no. 1, 2014)	11 Luxembourg (10)
2 Norway (2)	12 Canada (14)
3 Australia (5)	13 Finland (8)
4 Iceland (11)	14 South Korea (17)
5 Netherlands (13)	15 Czech Republic (16)
6 Sweden (4)	16 Belgium (12)
7 Denmark (6)	17 Japan (27)
8 Austria (3)	18 France (15)
9 Germany (7)	19 United States (19)
10 New Zealand (9)	20 Slovenia (21)

Natixis Global Asset Management, February 2015, http://ngam.natixis.com /docs/282/659/GRI%202015%20US%20News%20Release%20FINAL.pdf.

benefits. Some countries with "pay-as-you-go" systems are trying to build in a greater level of prefunding so that aging demographics don't make their plans unaffordable down the road. Nevertheless, in most cases the public retirement programs in most of these countries are more generous than what we have in the United States. And they act as an automatic stabilizer and economic stimulus that helps balance the overall economy, particularly during downturns.

As we have seen, the opponents and critics of Social Security, as well as of entitlements in general, have been willing to stretch the truth, spread misinformation, and spend whatever it takes to undermine these vital programs with the American public. Consequently, all of these phony claims and allegations keep springing to life, no matter how many times they are knocked down and shown to be as dead as a dinosaur. Instead of trying to diminish the importance of Social Security, we should increase and expand it so that it has a more robust foundation for Americans' retirement plans. Instead of obstructing Social Security from stepping into its crucially needed role as the nation's primary system of retirement income, we should take the next step in the natural evolution of our society that will allow us to maintain a vibrant middle class.

In the next chapter, I will present two proposals for how to greatly expand the Social Security payout for America's retirees, as well as how to pay for this expansion. One of these proposals shows how to double the current payout and make our retirement system fully portable. That's the type of bold step that our country needs. Our American nation is heading into an anxious era driven by a new, high-tech economy in which more workers will have to gain access to a portable safety net without the benefit of a single employer or a regular workplace. Many workers will have multiple employers, none of whom would be expected to provide much of a safety net under the current, antiquated model. If we are going to provide adequate resources for our retired seniors, we have to update, upgrade, and modernize our retirement system. In the next chapter, I show how we can do that.

CHAPTER FIVE

The Solution: Expanding Social Security

The Great Recession inflicted a lot of pain on many American households, and the recovery has been weak for all but the wealthiest, piling on to decades of wage and safety-net stagnation. In addition, the economic collapse was a catalyst in hitting "reset" on the US economy, flinging many occupations and industries toward a new and worrisome trajectory. More and more workers are losing the "good jobs" created by the New Deal economy, and instead are becoming contractors, freelancers, temps, and part timers in what is sometimes called the "new economy." Estimates vary, but it's clear that a high percentage of jobs are at risk of elimination from computers, robots, and artificial intelligence over the next twenty years—will those jobs be replaced by other forms of employment, just as when tractors replaced the horse and plow? No one really knows.[1] But many experts are growing concerned because already the quality and quantity of jobs has degraded in many occupations and industries, with less job security, lower wages, and a disappearing safety net.

Consequently, we as a nation are finding ourselves backed into a retirement corner. We have little choice but to view Social Security as an even more critical pillar of economic security. All Americans should have retirement benefits they can count on, not a casino of privatized 401(k)s run by the same Wall Street bankers and financial managers who drove the economy off the cliff in 2008. The three-legged stool of retirement security—Social Security, employer-based retirement plans, and private savings based on homeownership—has become wobbly and unstable. Despite all the "government *is* the problem" rhetoric that has pervaded US political discourse since the time of President Reagan, what's clear is that the privately held alternatives to Social Security have failed for most people. Those who keep proselytizing in their favor are like a drought-stricken farmer who keeps returning to the same dry well, hoping this time when he looks down the shaft, the outcome will turn out differently.

But it won't. Rather than hoping that private sources of retirement income will show better results or become more profitable in the future, we should reduce the reliance of most American workers on these unreliable schemes. We have to be pragmatic and evidence-based in making these assessments, and not blinded by rigid ideology. The best way—indeed, the only possible way, it seems—is to expand the popular, efficient, and successful Social Security system. While concern over too much "big government" is valid and real, the current failed system composed of hundreds of billions of dollars in federal subsidies going to wealthier Americans has the fingerprints of government all over it, too. The evidence is overwhelming that the public version of our retirement system has vastly outperformed the private system. Social Security emerges as the "least worst choice" for providing a degree of security for America's retirees. According to PBS *NewsHour*'s Philip Moeller, a retirement expert and coauthor of the bestselling book *Get What's Yours*, "What makes more sense—an expansion of a voluntary retirement savings program that hasn't worked well, or expansion of Social Security, which has worked well, is already available to nearly all workers, is very inexpensive to administer, and offers guaranteed payments that include inflation protection?"[2]

Social Security is now the only stable leg remaining that is reliably capable of delivering retirement security for tens of millions of Americans. In the decades ahead, the vast majority of baby boomers and other retirees will be almost completely dependent on the single leg of Social Security for their retirement. Social Security has become the nation's de facto national retirement system, *the* single pillar, a role for which it was never intended. As Moeller adds, "Social Security was never designed to be a provider of most of an older person's retirement income. But it has become so for most retirees. We need to recognize this reality as well as the limited success of the private retirement savings industry."[3]

There is only one major drawback to Social Security—currently its monthly payout to each individual is too low to play this fulcrum role. It has been designed to replace only about 30–40 percent of a worker's wages at retirement, but most financial advisors say that each individual will need approximately 70–80 percent of preretirement earnings in order to maintain a decent standard of living.[4] So the best solution is not only to expand Social Security, but in fact to double its monthly payout to each individual. That would bring us closer to a replacement level of around 60–80 percent, similar to the standard of national retirement systems in many other developed countries. Expanding Social Security into a more robust system of retirement income would result in a more secure workforce that enjoys complete portability when it comes to their individual retirement plans. Workers would be able to relocate in order to change jobs and not be worried about "job-lock," which plagues individuals who lose their pension benefit when they change jobs. That in turn would allow a degree of labor flexibility, which would contribute to better conditions for job creation. And it would unleash the natural genius of American workers, allowing them to work where they want instead of for the employer where they have the better retirement plan.

But will the public really get behind a plan to double the Social Security monthly benefit? I believe it will. Not only do polls show that the program is extremely popular, but those same polls indicate that a central reason the public supports Social Security is because they see it as an *earned* benefit. It's something all working Americans have paid into and believe they deserve to receive. Polls also show that Americans are in favor of expanding this extremely popular program. And why wouldn't they be in favor? The overwhelming evidence shows that it works. If, on top of that, the public recognizes how badly the private components of the retirement system have failed most Americans, the truth will create a powerful constituency for reform.

The Solution: "Social Security Plus"—Expanding Social Security

Social Security's monthly benefit should be expanded so that it provides approximately twice its current levels. The name I have given to this modified system of expanded benefits is Social Security Plus.

Currently, about 43 million retired seniors or their spouses are collecting retirement benefits, and the bill for providing those benefits to that senior population amounts to about $662 billion per year. So in order to double the current payout, we have to find another $662 billion.[5] That's a tall order, to be sure. But we can do it by making our tax system more *fair, innovative, and stable*—and more geared for today's modern economies. We need a way for workers to be able to pay into a portable and robust retirement system regardless of where they work, and when they finally retire, to receive a monthly benefit that is approximately double the current payout. Here's how we can do that.

Financing Social Security Plus could be accomplished in a number of ways. And its implementation could occur incrementally, in stages, which would ease any transition issues. As we will see, there are multiple possibilities for how to structure this, including for funding mechanisms. But the three best funding options come from modifying the US tax code in the following ways: (1) lift the unfair Social Security payroll cap currently in place, which taxes wealthy people at a much lower rate than middle- and working-class Americans; (2) eliminate tax subsidies granted to employers for sponsoring retirement plans; and (3) reduce, or even eliminate, the unfairness inherent in the tax code in general, which allows hundreds of billions of dollars in deductions that favor wealthier people over middle- and working-class Americans when it comes to investment, savings, housing, and more.

Let's look at each of these in turn.

Lift Social Security's payroll cap. As we saw in chapter 1, anyone making up to $118,500 a year in wage or salary has 6.2 percent of their wages for Social Security deducted from their paycheck (plus another 1.45 percent for Medicare); if they have an employer, the employer matches that amount, and if they are a contractor, free-lancer, or self-employed, they are responsible for paying the employer's half as well. While all Americans earning wage income are subjected to this rule, any income they earn over the $118,500 threshold is not taxed by Social Security. The net result of this is that working-, middle-, and even moderately upper-middle-class Americans, as well as their employers, are taxed the full rate of 12.4 percent on 100 percent of their income, but the wealthiest Americans are treated differently. They pay tax only on a portion of their income.

Hence, while a janitor's earnings of $35,000 per year are taxed the full 6.2 percent (with the employer paying another 6.2 percent), a corporate executive making $600,000 a year effectively is taxed at a rate of 1.2 percent of income. And millionaire bankers pay a paltry 0.73 percent of income (and neither the corporate exec or banker pay any Social Security tax at all on the considerable income they reap from investments, stocks, and dividends, known as capital gains—more on that later). The janitor is paying at least eight times the percentage of the banker. The banker is paying $55,000 less per year in Social Security payroll taxes than what he or she should be paying. So this payroll tax is very regressive.

Applying the same rules to everyone via a flat tax would be the *fair* thing to do—and increasingly it is the right thing to do. Many conservatives favor a flat tax on income, but for Social Security, suddenly they lose their enthusiasm. Yet higher-income workers and employers with large numbers of higher-income workers would have little to complain about because they have already been the beneficiaries of exceptionally large tax deductions in various ways (and like everyone else, they will benefit from a doubling of their monthly Social Security benefit).

Moreover, there is a precedent for removing this limitation on taxable earnings. Medicare used to have a cap on taxable earnings but no longer does. The wealthy have accepted that being fully taxed is fair when it comes to health care for seniors, even though it does not translate into additional benefits for them. As a candidate in 2008, President Barack Obama stated that he supported raising the cap on the Social Security tax to help fund the program, proposing a Social Security tax of 4 percent on the amount of any income earned over $250,000 per year.[6] That would have been a good step in the right direction—if he had ever gotten around to actually proposing it to Congress—but it still begs the question: *Why* should wealthy people earning over $250,000, or even those earning between $118,500 and $250,000, pay a lower rate of taxation than their house cleaners and auto mechanics?

So, requiring all income levels to pay their fair share—meaning a flat tax in which everyone pays the same percentage rate on all of their income, not just a small chunk of it—would make the system's financing less regressive. If we completely lifted the payroll cap, how much revenue would that generate toward our goal of finding another $662 billion? Quite a lot, it turns out.

According to the Center for Economic and Policy Research, there are approximately 9 million Americans (out of the approximately 145 million Americans in the labor force) who earned incomes above the $118,500 cap for Social Security payroll tax.[7] If all of that income is taxed at the same 12.4 percent rate (both the worker's and the employer's share) as those Americans making less than $118,500, that would raise about $135 billion for the retirement portion of the Trust Fund, year after year, according to data from Social Security's chief actuary.[8] So taxing all income brackets equally would raise a sizable chunk of the revenue needed to double the Social Security payout from the current 30–40 percent of an individual's final salary to 60–80 percent.

Eliminating the payroll cap is a very big deal, because so much wealthy income goes untaxed for Social Security purposes. Higher-income Americans already receive a larger Social Security monthly benefit than middle-income or low-income Americans. They receive the maximum benefit of around $2,660 per month, or $32,000 each per year. For a married, two-income couple (assuming both earn a high income), that would total nearly $64,000 a year together (if they began taking their benefits at sixty-six). Since we are looking to double the Social Security payout, higher-income individuals would receive up to $64,000 per year, and high-income couples around $128,000 a year—for the rest of their lives in retirement. So affluent people would be well compensated in return for the elimination of the payroll cap.

Some critics opposed to getting rid of the payroll cap have said that those wealthy people paying the full tax of 6.2 percent on all of their income should receive an even more enormous increase in their benefit, one commensurate with the higher amount of tax they are paying. That could amount to a Social Security benefit of hundreds of thousands of dollars per year, conceivably, for the very wealthy. But even private pensions are prohibited by law from giving extremely large benefits to high-salaried employees, so a rule limiting the annual benefit to $64,000 per individual would not be unusual.

By lifting the payroll cap, we have already raised a significant sum, $135 billion, toward our goal of $662 billion.

Eliminate employer tax exclusions for sponsoring retirement plans. With a doubling of the Social Security payout available to all Americans, employer-based pensions and 401(k)s become much less crucial to the retirement system. By implementing Social Security Plus, employers would be liberated from the responsibility of providing retirement for their employees. That also means it would no longer be necessary to provide to employers the substantial deductions they currently receive from the federal government for providing a retirement plan for their employees.

Not many people realize it, but every tax-paying American subsidizes the retirement plans provided by companies, even though a small minority of Americans—disproportionately the better-off—benefit from them.[9] This is accomplished via the tax code, which allows employers to exclude from their taxable income any contributions they make on behalf of their employees to their defined-benefit pensions and defined contribution 401(k)-type plans. This has the effect of lowering employers' taxes by billions of dollars. Employers also are allowed to exempt from their taxable income any costs they incur in the implementation and administration of a retirement plan. The employer can also shield from taxes any earnings it reaps from investing the funds stashed away in the company's pension/retirement fund. In other words, all pension/retirement contributions from employers are exempt from corporate income and Social Security payroll taxes (and most pension contributions an employer receives from employees are exempt from income tax as well).[10] These federal tax incentives are intended to motivate employers to sponsor retirement plans for their employees. The exemptions granted to qualified retirement plans are one of the largest tax expenditures in the federal budget, totaling some $113 billion in 2015.[11]

However, some of these employers also have to pay taxes when their employees start withdrawing their retirement benefits (because at that point the contributions are counted as income, and so both employer and employee pay the usual taxes associated with paid income, such as income, Social Security, and Medicare taxes). Still, after deductions, deferments, and tax payments are taken into account, employers still receive a hefty federal subsidy, which amounted to about $91 billion in 2015.

To be clear: although these federal subsidies are applied through the tax code, their effect is just the same as if the government were writing checks to deposit into the accounts of these companies that provide a retirement plan. That's why in official government tables, these subsidies are called "tax expenditures," because it's as if the government is spending tax dollars on these programs. These expenditures are used to encourage certain kinds of government-supported behavior by subsidizing it. Yet, because they are enacted through the tax code—reducing government revenue from what it otherwise would be, rather than appearing on the balance sheet as increased government spending—they mask the reality of what this is: it is a federal subsidy for companies that provide a pension/retirement plan for their employees, as well as an indirect subsidy of those employees.

As we have seen, most of the Americans who benefit from such private retirement plans have higher incomes. It's easy to criticize government programs for poor people and welfare recipients, because that appears in the budget—and in the media headlines—as government spending (on people who some view as undeserving). But in fact *more* tax dollars are spent on behalf of better-off Americans—that is, they are *more* subsidized than the poor—yet that is masked from the headlines and public scrutiny because it appears as exclusions, deductions, and deferrals, not as a budgetary spending item. These hidden subsidies are why economists like Mark Zandi have stated that tax expenditures should be considered a form of government spending.[12]

But if we are doubling the Social Security payout, all of these federal subsidies are no longer necessary. The vast majority of Americans would be better off if employers directed their pension money into a Social Security Plus system. It makes sense to remove the tax advantages and government guarantees provided to employers for their retirement plans, and to use this revenue instead to boost Social Security. By doing that we would raise about $91 billion for the Social Security Plus kitty in our bid to reach $662 billion. Combined with the previous $135 billion, we are a third of the way to our goal.

Eliminate tax shelters for 1-percenter households and businesses. The tax code is riddled with loopholes and labyrinths that only tax attorneys and accountants can figure out. Some of these loopholes have odd, technical-sounding names that most Americans have never heard of: "capital gains," "step-up in basis," and "carried interest."

Capital gains is the name given to profit made from investment income rather than wage-earned income, whether the investments come from real estate, investing in a business, or buying and selling in the stock market. As a way of encouraging business investment, the tax rates that are applied to *long-term* capital gains (defined as investments held for greater than a year) and dividends (made from investments such as stocks and bonds) are much lower than the rates for regular (wage- or salary-based) income. Someone earning a salaried income of $500,000 would be subject to the top income tax rate of 39.6 percent, but if they made that same $500,000 in the stock market or in real-estate investments, they are only taxed at a 20 percent rate (and in some cases even lower). Thus, they are paying half the taxes that the progressive income tax code calls for, and a lower tax rate than their mid-level managers or their doorman.

The Congressional Budget Office has estimated that this rule cost the federal treasury approximately $161 billion in 2013—and, surprise surprise—a whopping 93 percent of this subsidy is hoovered by Americans in the top 20 percent income bracket, and nearly 70 percent by the top 1 percent.[13] Making matters worse, the US Federal Reserve published a study that found that "unrealized capital gains" (the technical term given to capital income that has not yet been taxed) make up 55 percent of the total value of estates worth more than $100 million.[14] Economist Larry Summers coauthored a report that concluded, "More than half of the wealth accumulated within the richest estates has never been subject to income taxes."[15]

That's a lot of potential tax revenue lost due to the idiosyncrasies of the tax laws, which as recently as 1990 under President George H. W. Bush treated income from capital gains the same as any other type of income. But here's the thing: as outrageous as it sounds to tax capital gains at only half the rate of regular income, *none of this capital gains income is taxed for Social Security purposes at all.* Not a single dime from this type of investment income was deposited into the Trust Fund as a contribution toward the nation's retirement system. This is contrary to how other government programs work; for example, Medicare is partly funded by a 3.8 percent tax applied to the capital gains of higher-income taxpayers with adjusted gross incomes above $200,000 for single taxpayers and $250,000 for couples (who file jointly).[16]

Approximately $800 billion in capital gains income was earned in 2013. So, if that capital gains income had been taxed for Social Security purposes at the standard 6.2 percent, that would have generated around $50 billion for the Social Security Trust Fund. If we include the employer's half, that would generate another $50 billion.

OK, that's a lot of money, but there are other tax travesties that cause both the federal treasury and the Social Security Trust Fund to leak revenue. One of these has a name that sounds like an exercise workout that you might do at the gym: "step-up in basis."

But this is a tax exercise that only the wealthy are allowed to do. It's yet another tax shelter for the affluent that in fact functions as a direct federal subsidy for *inherited* wealth. Here's how it works.

Usually, when a home or a yacht or any other type of large expensive asset is sold, the seller realizes a capital gain, subject to the lower capital gains taxation rate of 15–20 percent (about half the tax rate of 39.6 percent that they pay on their earned income). Normally, the amount subject to taxation is the difference between the sale price and the amount that the seller originally paid for that particular asset. But it works differently for inherited property.

Instead of calculating the difference based on the amount originally paid, it's calculated using a more recent value, that of the "fair market value" of the asset on the date that the previous owner died and left it to his or her heirs. By doing this, the appreciation in value is far less, and hence, so are the capital gains taxes paid. Using this date of when the owner died, instead of its original sale price, is termed—bingo!—a "step-up in basis."

A better name for it might be a "step-up in privilege." Wouldn't it be lovely if all Americans could benefit from such an enormous inheritance loophole, rather than only the top 1 percent of 1 percent? In 2015, the step-up in basis rule reduced federal revenues by a whopping $63 billion.[17] That's a greater amount than the $42 billion spent on affordable housing programs for low-income people by the US Department of Housing and Urban Development. The Congressional Budget Office estimates that the step-up in basis rule will reduce federal revenues by $644 billion over the next ten years, with 21 percent of that subsidy going to the top 1 percent of income earners, and 65 percent going to the top 20 percent. The bottom 40 percent of income earners receive only 3 percent of these benefits.[18] Of the more than two hundred federal tax expenditures in the individual and corporate income tax systems, this is one of the ten largest. And yet this little loophole in the tax code labyrinth, which is hardly ever talked about, is an extremely lucrative subsidy for the wealthiest estates. And of course none of the income received from the sale of these large assets is taxed for Social Security purposes. If that at least were done at the 6.2 percent rate, it would generate another $19 billion for the Trust Fund.[19]

Some defenders of a low capital gains tax who view it as an incentive for business investment will cry foul over taxing investment income at the same rate as wages and salaries. But one special type of capital gains is hard to defend. It's called "carried interest."

Carried interest is a big chunk of the compensation paid to hedge fund managers, private equity executives, and venture capital partners. It is derived from taking a 2 percent fee for managing the billions of dollars from those who have invested in their hedge fund or stock portfolios. In addition, these managers are compensated by skimming off the top 20 percent of the profits made on their investment portfolios. According to the *New York Times*, because the "carry" is tied to performance, it is treated like an investment and subjected to the lower capital gains tax rate, rather than as ordinary income, even though most managers don't put any of their own money at risk.[20]

The people who benefit from this preferential tax treatment are among the richest in the country. In 2014, the top twenty-five hedge fund managers together earned nearly $12 billion—an average of $467 million each—which is more than the amount of federal food assistance received by over 4 million poor Californians.[21] According to the Internal Revenue Service, in 2012 the top four hundred earners in the United States, which includes a lot of hedge fund and private equity managers, paid the second-lowest average federal tax rate since the data has been collected, only 16.7 percent. Two decades ago, the "top 400" paid nearly 27 percent of their income in federal taxes. The change is mostly due to the fact that a lot more of their income is now taxed at the lower capital gains rate.[22]

Former GOP presidential candidate Mitt Romney, as a former hedge fund partner at Bain Capital, benefited from substantial carried interest on his 2010 and 2011 income tax returns, the *Boston Globe* reported, resulting in his paying an income tax rate of only 14 percent.[23] Victor Fleischer, a law professor at the University of San Diego and an expert on the carried-interest loophole, says, "It symbolizes how the 1 percent, or the one-tenth of 1 percent, can exploit the tax and legal system to their own benefit in ways ordinary people cannot." Adds Professor Fleischer, "If you're a teacher or a firefighter or a journalist, you can't transform your labor income into capital gains." But if you're a hedge fund manager, the Internal Revenue Service provides a posh loophole.[24]

Just closing this part of the capital gains loophole would raise a ton of money, though the estimates of how much vary greatly. Professor Fleischer estimates that the amount would be approximately $18 billion per year.[25] And during the run up to the 2016 presidential election, a most unlikely source emerged as the Robin Hood wanting to go after it: Donald Trump. In the heat of the GOP presidential primary, Trump announced that one thing he would do if elected is close the carried-interest loophole. "The hedge fund guys didn't build this country," Trump told John Dickerson on CBS's *Face the Nation.* "These are guys that shift paper around and they get lucky.... The hedge fund guys are getting away with murder."[26]

Jeb Bush, hardly a populist or one to buck the GOP establishment, soon jumped on the anti-carried-interest bandwagon. In September 2015, the *New York Times* wrote that Trump had "done more to put a stake in the heart of the carried-interest tax loophole in the last month than the Obama administration has in the last six and a half years."[27]

Again, it's important to note here that not only is the federal treasury missing out on billions of dollars in income tax, but even if the beneficiaries of this policy are allowed to keep that carried interest, none of this income is being subjected to a Social Security payroll tax. These capital gains buccaneers get off with making no contributions on their sky-high investment income into the Social Security Trust Fund. A conservative, back-of-the-envelope calculation suggests that approximately $90 billion in carried interest income was earned in 2014, and if that income had been subjected to the 6.2 percent Social Security payroll tax, plus another 6.2 percent for the employer's half, it would have yielded another $11.2 billion for Social Security.

So if we taxed long-term capital gains and dividends at the same rate as all other income, that would claw back *$161 billion* for the federal treasury, which can be put into the Social Security Plus kitty. And if we eliminated the "step-up in basis" rule for inherited wealth, that would add another *$63 billion* to the federal treasury. In addition, if all these different types of capital gains income are taxed for Social Security purposes at the 6.2 percent rate, as well as their employers where appropriate, that would add another *$100 billion* for capital gains, plus another *$19 billion* on the step-up in basis income and *$11.2 billion* for the carried-interest contribution to Social Security. Keep in mind, all I am doing in this exercise is taxing income derived from capital gains, carried interest, and step-up in basis in the same manner as how wages and salaries are taxed for the vast majority of Americans. What's fair for one is fair for all.

At this point, we have found some *$580 billion* in funding for Social Security Plus, simply by lifting the payroll cap, doing away with the tax subsidies given to employers for providing a retirement plan for their employees, and taxing the different forms of capital gains like regular income. That provides nearly 88 percent of the $662 billion in revenue needed to double the monthly retirement benefit. We have almost reached our mark, so let's keep going and look for more sources of revenue for our increasingly expanded and financially sound national retirement plan.

Reduce or Eliminate Other Unfair Deductions in the Tax Code That Disproportionally Benefit a Small Minority of Better-Off Americans

Another source of income for Social Security Plus would be to decrease or even eliminate many other deductions from the tax code that disproportionately favor upper-income people. As we saw in chapter 2, the US tax code has created a two-tier welfare state, in which better-off Americans benefit disproportionately from federal tax deductions and exclusions for private retirement savings and homeownership. These beneficiaries are positioned to take advantage of an enormous number of regressive components inlaid into our tax structure.

Financial instruments that encourage savings, including 401(k)s, 403(b)s, IRAs, and traditional pensions, are skewed toward helping better-off Americans. In fact, of the $165 billion that the federal government spends subsidizing individual retirement savings, nearly 80 percent of it goes to the top 20 percent of income earners. The middle class and poor can rarely take advantage of these deductions because they don't make enough income to participate.

And the same is true for federal subsidies of homeownership. The federal subsidy for the home mortgage interest deduction amounts to around $70 billion per year, with Americans in the top 10 percent income bracket hoovering a whopping 86 percent of this federal subsidy. And the federal tax deduction allowed to homeowners to mitigate the cost of state and local property taxes they pay on their houses cost the federal budget another $32 billion in 2014; a study by the Congressional Budget Office found that Americans in the upper 20 percent income bracket reaped 80 percent of this federal subsidy.[28] And just to make sure everyone paying attention understands who the tax code favors, homeowners also do not have to pay taxes on up to $250,000 of their capital gains profits when they sell their home, which doubles to $500,000 for married taxpayers. That exclusion amounted to a federal subsidy to the tune of another $52 billion in 2014. Together, these three federal subsidies for homeownership total $154 billion—and for the most part they subsidize higher-income taxpayers. Renters and most low-income people don't benefit at all, and while some middle-income people benefit, the total amount of their deductions and subsidies are comparatively small.

Changing these housing subventions that so grossly benefit politically powerful upper-income earners might seem legislatively impossible, yet it occurred in Germany in 1987. Germany once had a high rate of homeownership, but now its rate is below 50 percent (the rate in the United States is 65 percent, but before the housing bubble collapse in 2008 it was as high as 70 percent). The country eliminated its mortgage interest deduction along with other homeowner subsidies. Like Americans, homebuyers in Germany used to be able to deduct mortgage interest from their federal income taxes, but the country managed to eliminate that tax break under conservative chancellor Helmut Kohl.

About a decade later, in 2006, under conservative chancellor Angela Merkel, the country also eliminated a large-scale subsidy program for homeowners, amounting to about $12 billion per year.[29] While the United States is usually viewed as the land of laissez-faire, where markets rule and government intervention is low, it actually provides far more subsidy to its housing market than Germany, and most of it benefits better-off Americans. The United States clearly needs a new tax policy for housing, one that is rooted in a recognition of the unfairness built into the current tax code.

So, if we got rid of the subsidies for homeownership, and added that revenue to the Social Security Plus Trust Fund, that would amount to another $154 billion; if we also deep-sixed federal subsidies for individuals contributing money into their 401(k)s, pensions, and the like, which will not be needed anymore once we double the Social Security pension annuity, that would add another $165 billion to the fund.

If we combine those budgetary add-backs with our previous savings, we now have reached nearly *$900 billion*, well over the *$662 billion* level we needed to reach in order to enact Social Security Plus and double this highly popular national retirement system's payout. Just a few revenue streams—lifting Social Security's payroll cap, eliminating the employer tax deduction for providing a retirement plan, and eliminating some unfair deductions that vastly oversubsidize wealthier Americans—would raise more than enough revenue needed for creating Social Security Plus, which would provide a stable, secure retirement for every American. That's even enough revenue to take a major step toward covering the predicted Social Security shortfall in the 2030s, as well as the impending gap in funding for Social Security's disability fund. And we were able to do this without spending a dime more in government money or national wealth than what is *already being spent on the retirement system*. We are just shifting expenditures that right now benefit a small number of individuals and special interests as a result of how the tax code is structured, and re-focusing these resources on the vast majority of Americans.

Some tax and retirement experts will counter that eliminating the identified loopholes and exclusions will raise less federal revenue than it might appear because people will modify their behavior in response. Or some will object that eliminating all of these loopholes and deductions will raise revenues by less than the sum of all those individual expenditures, because if all of the loopholes and subsidies were gone, more taxpayers would claim the standard income tax deduction (instead of itemizing exclusions and deductions). Undoubtedly there is truth to those points, and more precise modeling would be helpful. Yet this proposal has identified nearly a trillion dollars—far in excess of the $662 billion target. It's certainly a good place to begin a badly needed discussion about how we can greatly expand the Social Security payout.

Thus, more tax fairness results in a Social Security Plus system that is both viable and fundable. With the deep cracks in America's retirement benefits revealed by the Great Recession, it is now also desirable and necessary.

Beyond that, what's truly eye opening about this exercise is how the tax code trumpets, loudly and brashly, that the rich are not like you and me. All of the exclusions, deductions, deferrals, and low tax rates being eliminated are ones that benefit a small minority of Americans. Most of these programs and savings instruments are hugely regressive because in most instances you have to earn a lot of income in order to take advantage of them. Or you have to receive your income through investments, such as in stocks and real estate, which most Americans don't have. Higher-income people not only have the wealth but also access to the technical and legal expertise that makes it all possible, resulting in them paying lower taxes on their reduced taxable income, or in some cases paying a lower tax rate.

So as much as opponents such as Peter G. Peterson like to label Social Security and Medicare as "entitlements," these tax code favoritisms are nothing more than entitlements for wealthier Americans. The current system perversely amounts to a hidden subsidy for better-off Americans at the expense of everyone else. These affluent recipients of federal largess are the true "welfare queens" because these advantages are mostly not available to middle- and lower-income Americans, especially to the working class, who rarely have enough income to divert for savings or investment. A phasing out of these various tax deductions, and gradually reducing the amount of private income that the wealthy can shelter from taxation, would result in more fairness, as well as more revenue available to convert Social Security into Social Security Plus.

An Alternative Funding Mechanism for Social Security Plus

One of the criticisms of this proposed plan is that raising the payroll tax on the full salary and wages of better-off Americans will hurt America's businesses. That's because these businesses also will have to pay a 6.2 percent payroll tax on the income above the $118,500 level. So, this would constitute what some label a "mandate" on business, which, like the word "entitlement," has acquired the reputation of being a sinful economic vice. As businesses are the job creators, opponents say, ultimately applying the payroll tax equally to all income brackets will backfire by reducing the number of jobs.

Yet there is no evidence of a link between taxation rates and economic growth. A 2011 study by economists Thomas Piketty, Emmanuel Saez, and Stefanie Stantcheva found no correlation between reductions in top tax rates and growth. Another study, conducted by William Gale and Andrew Samwick at the Brookings Institution, found no evidence that increased economic growth resulted from major tax cuts under President Reagan in 1981 or President George W. Bush in 2001 and 2003. Likewise, the study found no evidence of reduced economic growth from tax increases under President Bill Clinton in 1993. A study by Danny Yagan of one of the largest reductions to a capital tax rate—the 2003 dividend tax cut—showed zero change in corporate investment and no effect on employee compensation. As with top tax rates generally, changes in capital gains tax rates are not correlated with a corresponding shift in economic growth.[30]

Yet still these myths persist. Of course, those same critics had little negative to say all these years as the payroll tax was levied on

100 percent of wages for middle- and lower-income Americans. When the reforms of the Greenspan Commission in the early 1980s raised the payroll tax rate from 5.4 percent to the current 6.2 percent (which was phased-in over several years), those same critics said it was a fiscally responsible thing to do. US businesses have somehow survived paying the 6.2 percent payroll tax on the full wages for the 110 million working Americans whose entire earnings are subject to the payroll tax. Only now that it would be applied to millions of wealthier Americans do the doomsayers say it will be bad for the economy and hurt job creation. I find these sorts of arguments disingenuous.

Nevertheless, to demonstrate the many ways that exist to finance a significant expansion of the monthly payout for Social Security Plus, here is an alternative way to structure it without raising the payroll tax beyond current levels. This proposal, which is based on one I coauthored with Michael Lind and Joshua Freedman from the New America Foundation and Robert Hiltonsmith from Dēmos, expands the public pillar of retirement income in a way that is consistent with the goal of making the nation's retirement system more robust, fully portable, and building on what we know has worked, instead of what has failed.

In this proposal, the current hybrid "public and private" system, which, as we have seen, is based on the three-legged stool of retirement security, would be replaced with a two-part, wholly public system. Just as Medicare already has different components called Medicare A, B, C, and D, this form of Social Security Plus would have two distinct parts. The first part, Social Security A, would be similar to the current Social Security program, which provides a retirement benefit based on earnings and the number of years worked. Those who earn more and work longer receive a greater monthly benefit than others. The second part would be a new universal flat benefit, Social Security B, funded by various mechanisms other than a payroll tax (which I will elaborate in a moment). It is intended to be redistributive—to prevent poverty in old age—and to ensure that retirees achieve some minimum standard of living.[31]

This kind of program, which is used in many other countries, has sometimes been referred to as a "double-decker" system, since it combines a basic flat public pension with a defined-benefit annuity based on earnings.[32] By using these two parts like a kind of seesaw, adjusting one part in relation to the other, it's possible to design a payout schedule in which, when Social Security A and B are pooled, most workers would be guaranteed around 60 percent of their average working wage in retirement income (compared to the current 30–40 percent of replacement income for the average worker). That would amount to a significant expansion of retirement income.

How would this double-decker system be financed? The two components of this plan for Social Security Plus would be paid for by separate revenue streams. Social Security A would be paid for by payroll taxes, just the way it works now, and at the same tax rate as the current program. But Social Security B, the new universal, flat benefit, would be financed by revenues other than payroll taxes—either from general revenues allocated by Congress as part of the budgetary process, or by a separate tax dedicated to Social Security B.

This is not as big of a change as it might seem. It's very similar to how Medicare already works, since slightly more than half of Medicare benefits are paid for by general revenues. As we saw earlier, Medicare is also partly funded by a 3.8 percent tax on capital gains of higher-income taxpayers. It's also similar to how Supplemental Security Income (SSI) is funded; SSI is a means-tested antipoverty program that helps poor children and the disabled, as well as the elderly, and it has always been funded out of general revenues. Medicare and SSI thus provide a precedent for expanding the funding base for Social Security out of general revenue funds. In fact, we could even convert SSI into Social Security B, and then expand it with more revenue commensurate with the greater role it would be taking on, which would further simplify the overall program.

Where will Congress get the money for Social Security B? The whole thing could be funded from the revenue sources identified in the previous plan: by closing the capital gains loopholes and by ending or at least greatly reducing the exclusions and deductions that disproportionately advantage better-off Americans. That would include ending or reducing subsidies for 401(k)s and pensions (both for businesses and their employees), for various home ownership deductions, for inherited wealth, and for capital gains income from investments. We could also levy a small financial transaction tax on the buying and selling of stocks and bonds; with millions of transactions bought and sold every day, this would raise an estimated $200 billion. It also would disincentivize speculative trading via "black box" algorithms, which automatically launch millions of transactions per second and have caused wild roller-coaster rides on Wall Street of stocks plunging in a matter of seconds.[33]

All of this would result in much more progressive outcomes. As with the previous proposal, the highest-income earners would have to contribute their fair share to Social Security and would no longer be able to rely on their tax-favored federal subsidies. However, they would still receive a higher level of public retirement benefits than they do currently because of the addition of Social Security B, to which every American would be entitled.

Parts A and B together would provide a much greater share of retirement income than today's Social Security does by itself. This would further provide a sensible reason to make 401(k)s, employer-based pensions, and other tax-favored individual deductions less necessary, and to redirect those federal tax expenditures into revenues that can be used to pay for this version of Social Security Plus. For persons with no earnings or very irregular earnings, Social Security B would provide at least a minimum monthly benefit to ensure no American falls through the floor of a livable quality of life. Replacing tax-favored private retirement programs with a substantial expansion in the public portion of the national retirement system would make the program as a whole more progressive, efficient, and stable.

Some critics contend that the public will never support another social insurance program that depends so substantially on general revenue. But if that is really the case, then public support for Medicare should be weaker than it is. On the contrary, Medicare enjoys strong public support, along with Social Security.

Their popularity arises from the great need for them, and the perceived as well as the actual benefits, rather than from the specific details of how we pay for them. Americans value these programs, and poll after poll has shown that they are willing to see their taxes used for this purpose, even if it means paying higher taxes. Designed properly, a new retirement system could substantially boost retirement benefits and economic security for most Americans, even while costing the nation no more than the current amount devoted to retirement. Some version of this "double-decker" public system is already being used in many countries, including Japan, Canada, Belgium, Finland, South Korea, Switzerland, the United Kingdom, Luxembourg, and elsewhere.[34] All of these places utilize both a basic flat public pension and a public defined-benefit annuity program based on earnings.[35]

As this and the previous plan show, we can replace a wobbly stool and its failing private components with a single, sturdy, portable, and purely public column made up of a strong pillar of Social Security. No component in either of these plans is contingent on benefits provided by particular employers, all are portable from job to job. By replacing the status quo of employer-provided, tax-favored retirement savings plans with either of these proposed Social Security plans, we would create a portability that completely delinks the retirement income of individual Americans from particular jobs and employers. And that would help American businesses trying to compete with foreign companies that don't have to directly provide pensions to their employees, because those countries already have national retirement plans. The single pillar of Social Security Plus would go a long way toward preparing US workers and businesses for the new economy in the twenty-first century.

Responding to Criticisms

Some people reading this will no doubt mourn the loss of their own favorite tax deductions and personal subsidies. Certainly, some of these deductions have helped many people reach for their own version of the American dream. But take heart, perhaps we won't have to eliminate all of them from the tax code—

the first proposal identified sources of revenue for Social Security Plus that are almost twice as great as the need. So perhaps some of these entitlements for better-off Americans could just be scaled back a bit. But it's clear from this exercise that we must urgently reevaluate how to better target these subsidies at the greatest need. There are different ways to restructure some of these programs, with one possibility being to treat capital gains as income that is subject to a Social Security contribution (like they already are for Medicare); or to direct a small financial transaction tax on all stock market transactions into the Social Security Trust Fund. We could also eliminate the provision that allows taxpayers aged sixty-five and older to claim an additional standard deduction on their income tax returns, which reduced federal tax revenues by an estimated $2.7 billion in 2015.[36] This special deduction won't be necessary anymore, because these retirees already will be receiving twice their current Social Security payout.

While he was still living, Robert Ball, the former commissioner of Social Security who served under three presidents (Kennedy, Johnson, and Nixon), argued in favor of devoting the proceeds of an estate tax to Social Security. The tax perhaps would apply only to large estates of $3.5 million or more.[37] Still another possibility would be to use a flexible payroll tax, as Finland has done, in which payroll taxes are increased when the economy is going well and reduced when the country is hit by hard times. Such a counter-cyclical intervention acts as an automatic stabilizer to reduce the cost to employers of hiring workers during tough times, but during good times directs increased payroll-tax revenues toward a "rainy day fund" that can be deployed when needed.[38] A flexible payroll tax in the United States could deposit the extra revenues collected during prosperous years into a fund that helps finance an expansion of Social Security.

If Congress, after enacting a version of Social Security Plus, still wanted to promote private savings for middle-income Americans who can afford it, it could create a parallel system of simple, universal private retirement accounts with strict contribution limits that are more efficient and equitable than the failed 401(k) system. Every American with sufficient savings would be able to invest in government treasuries and other low-risk investments via this parallel plan of defined contributions. Like index funds, individual's savings would be pooled, and the resulting economies of scale would lower management fees and other administrative costs.

That's the rationale behind labor economist Teresa Ghilarducci's proposal for Guaranteed Retirement Accounts (GRAs) and Senator Tom Harkin's proposal for Universal, Secure, and Adaptable (USA) Retirement Funds, as well as proposals calling for all Americans, not just federal employees, to be allowed to invest in the federal government's Thrift Savings Plan.[39] All of these plans, like any insurance policy, allow risk sharing and minimize administrative costs by creating large pools of savings that are invested in low-risk investments. The GRAs and USA Retirement Funds are designed to protect savers against the tumult of stock market fluctuations by guaranteeing an annual rate of return (about 2 percent) and paying out a small annuity for most income earners. Crucially, however, adding a private retirement savings component to Social Security Plus would need a cap on contributions so that the program helps middle-income earners without becoming an unaffordable subsidy for wealthier Americans, like the 401(k) system has become.[40]

Social Security Plus also could be implemented in stages, targeting expanded benefits first to those who are most in need. For example, the conversion could begin by first focusing on the most needy—increasing the minimum Social Security benefit for the bottom 25 percent of seniors, most of whom live in poverty.[41] Another option would be to allow active seniors over sixty-two years of age who have not yet reached full retirement age (sixty-six years old) to take a half pension and work half time without losing their right to a full pension upon their retirement. That would both reduce the strain on the Social Security system and ensure that seniors could ease their way into retirement while building up savings, clearing the way for younger people to find jobs.

If nothing else, it should be apparent from these examples that multiple funding mechanisms and implementation plans are possible toward the desired goal of providing retirement security for all Americans. It's a matter of priorities and politics, not affordability or complex design.

Of course, all Americans should review these proposals and consider how they would affect their own individual and family circumstances. Ending public subsidies for employer-provided, defined-benefit pensions might raise concerns for some labor unions, which normally are natural allies to the idea of expanding Social Security. But I would argue that union members will gain far more by having a doubling of their retirement payout, and also by having employers relieved of that retirement responsibility (other than paying their employer contribution for each worker into Social Security), making that one less contentious issue subject to contract negotiations and collective bargaining. This would allow unions to focus more on wages and other benefits.

Some opponents of entitlements and Social Security will no doubt protest that this reformatting of the nation's retirement system will hurt the overall economy. But nothing could be further from the truth. I have demonstrated how we could pay for it, so it is not going to add a penny to the debt. It's just reallocating current national wealth more efficiently, and targeting it more directly at the nation's retirement needs. Far from hurting the economy, reducing these tax advantages for the better-off will help the economy in a number of ways. An expansion of Social Security payouts would have a permanent stimulating effect on the economy because, as most economists know, low- and middle-income people are more likely to spend an extra dollar on goods and services than are affluent individuals. Non-wealthy people need to spend that money for their daily needs and ultimately for their retirement; better-off Americans tend to save the income. And as we have seen, contrary to conservative belief, there is little evidence that wealthy savers are job creators, or that they somehow use their surplus resources to grow the economy. They simply save their private wealth and then will it to their heirs.

Social Security Plus also would act as an automatic stabilizer during economic downturns and ensure that even when the economy is merely plodding along, retirees will still have a decent enough income. And by redirecting wealth from 401(k)s, pensions, the stock market, and other speculative activities, it also would discourage investment asset bubbles from developing in the future, which is a net positive since bubbles are very destabilizing when they burst.

In fact, it would be better if the new sources of revenue for Social Security Plus are invested in US treasuries, rather than the status quo of employers investing their pension funds—or employees their 401(k)s—in the stock market, and paying exorbitant fees to financial managers, most of whom can't even beat the Dow Jones average for returns. Directing the investments into "Social Security Treasuries" would contribute to a system that better ensures more Americans against economic downturns, since the full faith and credit of the US government would be standing behind the promised benefits. Average Americans would not have to accumulate their own stockpile of financial assets to tide them over during a downturn, because their retirement security would be backstopped by these "Social Security Treasuries." Workers wouldn't have to pay manager fees that drain their pension funds, nor would they have to assume all that investment risk.

And because the doubling of the Social Security payout would be universal, even those better-off Americans who are losing their tax exclusions, deductions, and deferrals would see at least part of it returned back to them in the form of a much greater payout from Social Security. This would considerably simplify our tax code and our retirement system. It would be a win-win for the nation.

What we have seen is that it is possible to expand Social Security in a way that would greatly stabilize American workers' retirement plans, as well as the national retirement system as a whole *and* also the broader macroeconomy. Indeed, the entire history of Social Security, stretching back to its founding in the late 1930s, can be viewed as an ever-evolving part of not only the social contract but the stability of the macroeconomy itself. This latest evolution would just take it to the next step along its destiny, laying an even more robust foundation for the nation as a whole.

Guaranteeing the American Dream Through Social Security Plus

A woman I know named Jessica lost her job during the Great Recession, one of millions of casualties of the biggest economic collapse since "the one whose name must not be mentioned" (psst . . . the Great Depression). She had worked as a secretarial assistant for an upper-crust law firm in downtown San Francisco, which provided health care, a company pension, and decent wages. But when the economic earthquake shook, suddenly her world came crashing down. She was laid off and entered the scary, new world of being marginally employed.

Still in her mid-thirties, she collected unemployment for six months and then she bumped around from job to job, working as a temp, freelancer, contractor, gig-preneur—just about every worker classification there is—mostly part time with an occasional full-time office gig that lasted a short time. She tried her hand at being an Uber driver ("the company treats you like you are gum on the bottom of their shoe," she said), and then she did a stint as a TaskRabbit handygal ("being called a 'rabbit,'" she explained, "reminded me too much of Michael Moore's film *Roger and Me*, when laid-off autoworkers ate pet rabbits being sold for food"). Finally, sick of feeling like a tumbleweed in the labor market, she scraped together her savings, borrowed a little from family and friends, and launched her own business. She decided to pursue a dream of being a seamstress, designing her own local line of women's wear. She could use a "sharing economy" company like Etsy and its app-driven platform to advertise and sell. What the heck, she thought; if someone can make a fortune making cupcakes, why can't I succeed at doing something I enjoy?

But soon after launching her one-woman business, she discovered that this was no nine-to-five gig. Oftentimes her workday was long, fifteen hours or more, sewing during the day and promoting her business at night, by e-mail, on her web page (which she maintained herself), often chained to her computer into the wee hours of the night. Working out of her apartment, slowly she cobbled together a small client list, mainly of older affluent women, silver-haired ladies with Margaret Thatcher hairdos who could afford her services. Though often these clients were so demanding of her time that when she figured out her earnings based on the number of hours worked, sometimes she barely made minimum wage. Plus, now she had to pay for her own health care, she had no paid vacations or holidays, and if she got sick, she couldn't afford to take a day off. She knew she should be putting a certain amount of earnings away in order to build up her savings, but she didn't earn enough to do that. She knew she was required, by law, to pay both her Social Security and Medicare contributions as well as the employers' share, a total of 12.4 + 2.9 percent (15.3 percent) of her meager income, but that bite was kind of big, so sometimes she fudged on paying that as well.

Eventually she had to take a part-time job in order to make ends meet. After a couple of years of existing this way, she began focusing more intently on finding another full-time job, while still trying to service her small client list. As the economy began to recover somewhat, companies were hiring again, but now there was not as much of a demand for her office skills. New productivity software could do a lot of what she used to do. Should she go back to school and get more training, she wondered? She still had to pay off her original student loans. All of these questions rolled around in her head, nagging, as she worked over the sewing machine in her apartment.

For Jessica, and millions of workers like her, these dilemmas plague their every working day. Jessica used to converse with her wealthy lady clients, in the midst of measuring and sizing them, and they would give her advice about her business: "*Deductions, Jessica,*" they would tell her. "*That's the key, deductions.*" If only she had a dollar for every time she heard that word. She was amazed to hear them talk about all their tax deductions and shelters, whether on their husbands' business expenses (such as "work meetings" on the French Riviera), or the mortgage deductions on their fabulous homes in Seacliff or Pacific Heights, or on their 401(k)s and IRAs, or the low tax rate they paid on their capital gains investment income, and the accountant tricks with strange names like "step-up in basis" that allowed them to significantly reduce their tax burden. As a budding businesswoman, Jessica was all in favor of deducting expenses—except her business income was so low that deductions did her little good.

One day it struck Jessica: All of these ladies have ways to deduct, defer, exclude, and lessen their tax burden, but someone such as herself does not. When she worked at the law firm, she didn't qualify for any deductions, outside the standard personal deduction that everyone is allowed on their income taxes. She was a renter, not a homeowner, so she didn't qualify for the home mortgage interest deduction; she had paid into her company pension, but couldn't afford a 401(k) or IRA, which would have qualified her for a tax-deferred deduction (and, as it turned out, her company received a significant federal subsidy for providing her pension). She didn't have any inheritance or capital gains income that would benefit from the various federal subsidies provided to those forms of income. And her business did not have enough revenue to significantly benefit from business deductions. It kind of angered her to realize that, the way the tax system is structured, *she*, Jessica, was subsidizing all these wealthy ladies and their mountains of deductions, exclusions, deferrals, and government subsidies. What's wrong with this picture? she wondered. Where is the fairness?

This is the nationwide context in which the debate over Social Security is taking place, yet most Americans don't even realize it. The tax system has become so unfair that's it's wealthier Americans who are today's "welfare queens," not the poor. As we have seen, many of America's most lucrative social welfare benefits relating to home ownership and retirement, as well as education and child care, are delivered through the tax codes as deductions against income. This has created a two-tiered welfare state that heavily favors higher-income groups; indeed the majority of benefits now go to the top 10–20 percent of wealthiest Americans, not to those who need them most.

But that also means that as unemployment and underemployment rise and the incomes of those in the middle decline, so do their benefits for education, child care, and retirement. As a result, many everyday Americans can quickly find themselves pushed into the lower tiers of America's social welfare system, fighting for limited resources.

Like many other Americans, at this point I find myself nostalgic for the "good old days," even as I realize that they were not so good. When I was a kid, *The Waltons* was a hit TV show about a farming family and its feel-good experiences during the Great Depression in a close-knit agrarian community in rural Virginia. Each episode ended warmly with "Good night, John-Boy." But today, when you say "The Waltons," it has a very different meaning—they are the controversial owners of a multinational retail corporation that operates a chain of discount department and warehouse stores. The heirs of Walmart founder Sam Walton— three children and one daughter-in-law—are worth collectively over $140 *billion* and ranked six, seven, nine, and ten on *Forbes*'s list of wealthiest Americans.[1] And yet Walmart officials insist that the scourge of just-in-time scheduling, in which employers dictate to their workers their daily work schedule, with no employee input or even advance notice, is central to its successful business model.[2] Walmart, which costs taxpayers $6.2 billion per year for providing public assistance to its workers because the pay is so low, accepts no criticism of its exploitative business practices.[3]

The ridesharing octopus Uber, which is headquartered in San

Francisco, raised eyebrows a few years ago over the Fourth of July weekend when it offered wealthy New Yorkers the "ultimate freedom from the crowds, the traffic and the long trip out East" to the exclusive enclave of the Hamptons: a rented helicopter for $3,000, called UberCHOPPER. "Blair Waldorf, Don Draper and Jay Gatsby got nothing on you. This is the epitome of luxury, convenience and style," Uber boasted in a blog post.[4]

And billionaire Facebook executive and Napster founder Sean Parker spent $10 million on his fantasy wedding in a redwood forest on California's Big Sur coast, hiring a landscaping company to "modify" the forest. The California Coastal Commission said Parker hadn't acquired the permits for such modifications and ordered him to shut the party down. But Parker ignored the commission and went ahead anyway. The wedding took place amidst fake fairyland castle-type ruins, an artificial waterfall, stone bridge, and elfin cottage surrounded by five-hundred-year-old giant redwoods. In attendance was an A-list of guests that only money can attract, including entertainment glitterati such as Sting, *Harry Potter*'s Emma Watson, Sean Lennon, and Metallica drummer Lars Ulrich. Democratic politicians such as California attorney general Kamala Harris, former San Francisco mayor Gavin Newsom, and now-US senator Cory Booker were also there, and reportedly all the guests were clad in custom-made Tolkienesque garb.[5] Afterward Parker paid a $2.5 million "settlement" to the coastal commission for his violations, but that's just pocket change for an arrogant billionaire.[6]

Not to be outdone, David Sacks, a former PayPal executive who founded Yammer, threw himself a birthday party rumored to cost $1.4 million. It had a Louis XVI theme, "Let him eat cake," complete with attendees dressed in Louis XVI costumes and entertained by Snoop Dogg.[7] Could there be a more fitting symbol for these extravagant times?

But it's not just certain rich individuals who have benefited from this new Gilded Age; it's also US corporations writ large. These "artful dodger" corporations have found numerous loopholes and foreign tax havens to reduce their tax liabilities.[8] On their $2.1 trillion in profit in 2013, they paid just $419 billion in

corporate taxes, an effective tax rate of just under 20 percent[9]—
one of the lowest rates since 1931, only a third of the rate that
corporations paid in the 1960s, and less than the rate paid by most
middle-class people.[10] The share of federal tax revenues paid by
US corporations has declined dramatically, from 33 percent in
1952 to a mere 11 percent today. Corporate profits are at their
highest level in at least eighty-five years, while employee compensation is at its lowest level in sixty-five years.[11]

So, it's pretty hard to argue with a straight face that our great
nation doesn't have the money to pay for a doubling of the Social
Security payout. Disparities in wealth, which have long been a
major part of the political jousting field on the American landscape, were greatly exacerbated by the Great Recession, and in
so many ways our nation has still not recovered. But it's getting
harder to notice, as the "new normal" has settled into our bones.
The economic collapse reinforced America's growing two-tier
society and put into question our entire economic model. It also
put enormous strain on the US social contract. A census report
found that many households have still not regained the purchas-
ing power they had before the recession that began in December 2007. Median household income was 6.5 percent lower in
2014 than in 2007, and with median household income in the
United States stuck at around $53,660 per year, that represents a
loss of nearly $3,500 per year, per household. Nearly 15 percent of
Americans remain in poverty, which amounts to almost 47 million people, larger than the entire populations of Spain, Kenya,
or Iraq.[12]

In the immediate aftermath of the economic collapse, in December 2009, the official unemployment rate was 10 percent, but
everyone knew that number was only a half-truth; even more
workers had dropped out of the labor force and become "dis-
couraged," and still others were forced into part-time work out of
necessity. Indeed, what is known as the U6 unemployment rate,
which is the measure for "total unemployed, plus all marginally
attached workers, plus total employed part time for economic
reasons," was over 17 percent for many months after the Great
Collapse. Today, the official unemployment rate is 5.7 percent,

but the U6 rate is still an alarming 11.3 percent.[13] There are a lot of workers who have left the labor force—an estimated 12 million, in fact—and other Americans who are stuck in part-time work.

And this occurred *after* two long decades of stagnant wages and declining prospects for the middle- and lower-income classes. The Great Recession clearly exposed the many holes in America's rather porous social safety net. Before the collapse, says Sherle Schwenninger, director of the Economic Growth Program at the New America Foundation, "rising home prices and access to credit had masked the effects of stagnating wages." Inflated prices (that we now know were the result of a massive housing bubble) allowed homeowners to live a fiction, maintaining and even improving their living standards by taking out second mortgages and tapping into the inflated equity in their homes. In addition, easy access to credit allowed families to weather economic downturns or medical emergencies. But it came at a slowly creeping cost—rising household indebtedness.

"With the bursting of the housing and credit bubble," Schwenninger explains, "this essential feature of the Clinton-Bush era imploded, leaving many households with a large debt hangover."[14]

The "New Economy" Steamroller Arrives

If only we could have frozen things there for a few years as we tried to figure out appropriate policy interventions. But rust never sleeps, and in the aftermath of the Great Recession, the economy morphed into another animal entirely—and in ways that make expanded Social Security even *more* important to the retirement security of most elderly Americans.

Increasing numbers of workers now find themselves on shaky ground, turned into freelancers, temps, contractors, and part timers. Even many professional jobs are experiencing this precarious shift. Within a decade, it's been estimated that nearly half of the 145 million working Americans could be impacted, turned into so-called "independent workers" with little job security, insufficient safety-net supports, and poor wages.[15] Add to that new antiworker methods such as "just-in-time" scheduling and the steamroller of automation, robots, and artificial intelligence already replacing millions of workers and projected to "obsolesce" millions more, and suddenly things don't look so economically set for a lot of Americans. Now an insidious mash-up of Silicon Valley technology and Wall Street greed has thrust upon us the latest economic trend: the so-called "sharing economy," with companies that offer short-term freelancer employment with low pay, no safety net, and a need to be in constant job search mode, looking for the next gig. One Uber driver with whom I spoke laughed bitterly when I mentioned the term "sharing economy." "More like the 'share the crumbs' economy," he said.[16]

It's an alarming transformation. The US middle class, one of America's greatest inventions and a gift to the world, is in danger. The future is anything but secure. Set to replace the crumbling New Deal society is a darker world in which workers can be hired and fired by the touch of an app—turned on and off like a water spigot.

These changes mark one of the great social and economic transformations of the postwar era. A seismic shake to the supportive edifice for American workers has cracked and is beginning to crumble for all but the better-off. Not since the Great Depression have we been so in need of a system of retirement security that acts as both a buffer for individuals and families from the sudden shocks of economic downturns and bursting asset bubbles, but that also acts as an automatic stabilizer and stimulus capable of steadying the broader macroeconomy. At the very time when Americans most need a stable retirement system, it is more threatened than ever.

So yes, our economy is changing, and yes, Social Security must change with the times. But the change that must occur is not cutting it back, quite the contrary. We have to expand Social Security and create a robust, single pillar retirement system for every worker, one that is portable from job to job. And one that functions even for those workers who have multiple employers. So the safety net has to work for these new types of workers, and for many different classifications of workers. That's what the need is, and an expanded Social Security could best provide the retirement portion of this new kind of safety net for this new kind of economy. No other system or method—not 401(k)s, IRAs, the remnants of company pensions, the loopholes of tax deductions and deferrals, or any other current method, even if scaled up—are capable of playing this role. Only Social Security can do it.

And yet Social Security's payout to each individual is so meager that, unless it is expanded, it will not be robust enough to play this central role as the nation's de facto national retirement system.

Social Security Plus—the Only Solution Left Untried

Winston Churchill allegedly once said, "You can always count on Americans to do the right thing—after they have tried everything else."[17] We've tried just about everything else to create a secure retirement system for seniors, and to stabilize this part of the consumer demand that drives our economy. What we haven't yet tried is Social Security Plus.

Late nineteenth-century German leader Otto von Bismarck first pioneered the idea of old-age government pensions, and it has since become a staple around the world. A universal social support system, whether in Europe, Canada, Japan, or Australia, is guided by a philosophy that values the creation of "social insurance" that helps individuals and families prepare for their future, including retirement. In fact, the various social insurance systems *force* individuals to prepare, paycheck by paycheck, by deducting from workers and businesses the funds necessary to better secure their futures. Universal social insurance means everyone pools their money, which is a crucial step that allows better planning and the creation of more efficient and less expensive support systems. Consequently, European systems of health care, child care, senior care, housing, and education cost much less per capita compared to US systems, because the efficiencies that can be designed into universal systems make them much more economical and cost-effective.

For example, the United States spends over 17 percent of gross domestic product (GDP)—about $2.9 trillion, or $9,255 per person—on a decentralized hodgepodge health-care system that is very expensive to administer and operate.[18] Even after the improvements of Obamacare, health care still doesn't cover about 11 percent of the US population. But European nations spend about 6–12 percent of GDP (depending on the country) and cover 100 percent of their populations.[19] Americans also spend at least six times more per capita for child care (depending on the country), and while university tuition is skyrocketing in the United States, in most European nations it is still quite inexpensive, only a few hundred dollars per year.[20]

The Swedish Social Insurance Agency publishes a brochure that captures the prevailing philosophy: "Social insurance is founded on the idea of people helping each other through a kind of social safety net, which is in place from birth to retirement."[21] Netherlands Labor Party leader Wouter Bos has argued that Europe's social state is based on "enlightened self-interest" since "we all run the same risks, so we might as well collectively insure ourselves against those risks."[22] This is a philosophy with broad agreement across the political spectrum; even conservatives and the so-called far right agree, forming the basis for a "European consensus."

So enacting a version of Social Security Plus is not as untested as it may at first appear. In many nations around the world, more comprehensive social support systems aid families and individuals and cushion vulnerable populations against economic dislocation. Nevertheless, in the United States we continue stumbling forward with our more ad hoc, decentralized, and inefficient systems, in which some people get the support they need and others don't. And the support systems are so poorly designed that the national price tag is often exorbitantly expensive. The more deregulated US system is known for allowing individuals to keep more of their paycheck—presidents from Ronald Reagan to George W. Bush were famous for declaring, "We let you keep your own money"—and leaves it up to Americans' discretion whether to prepare for the long run by saving money and handling the costs of retirement, or to spend it all in the short run. But in an age of globalized capitalism and increasing economic insecurity, benefits like an adequate retirement, as well as health care, child care, sick leave, education, housing, and more, are no longer discretionary—they are *necessary* in order to enjoy a basic level of security and comfort. What this points to is that in today's insecure age, a middle-class standard of living is not only about income levels or economic growth rates, but also about adequate support institutions and social insurance for individuals and families.

Japan, Canada, and countries in Europe and elsewhere have already established various vehicles to ensure their health, productivity, and quality of life that will serve them well in the new, high-tech economy. While all of these nations, like the United States, rely on powerful capitalist engines as the core wealth generator of their economies, the presence of a more robust social insurance infrastructure is the reason that these other nations have a higher level of economic security for its people than does the United States. The US is the outlier among developed nations; our "ownership society" should be called an "on-your-own" society because many people are truly left on their own.

The security of social insurance in turn stimulates consumer spending, which in turn creates jobs, which in turn acts as an automatic stabilizer during downturns. It unleashes a virtuous feedback loop, based on these necessary components of a modern capitalist economy today. A more comprehensive social insurance system allows these other countries' to achieve one of America's chief principles, namely, "life, liberty, and the pursuit of happiness," with results that are vastly different from the American "pull yourself up by your bootstraps" society. Expanding Social Security would be an important step toward providing for all Americans the type of efficiencies that modern capitalist economies need in order to provide retirement security.

One can anticipate various objections, criticisms, and even fear of creating a Social Security Plus system. *"It has never been tried before"* (at least not in the United States), *"it's socialism"* (even though 70 percent of Republicans support Social Security), *"it's already going bankrupt"* (nonsense), and *"where would we find the money?"* (how about from all the hundreds of billions of dollars in tax loopholes that predominantly favor wealthier Americans?). Already there exists a concerted and well-funded effort to convince Americans that Social Security is broken and that we need to cut it back and even privatize it "in order to save it." So I'm very aware that some Americans, both leaders and everyday citizens who have grown so suspicious of government, will reject out of hand the notion of doubling the monthly benefit.

But what can't be denied, as this book has demonstrated, is that the "three-legged stool" of retirement security in the United States has become wobbly and unstable. Two of the legs—private, employer-based retirement plans, and private savings based on homeownership—have nearly collapsed. Combine that with vast increases in inequality, flat wages, and a decline in personal savings in the years even before the Great Recession, and Social Security is now the only leg standing for tens of millions of Americans. An expansion of Social Security—one of the most successful and popular government programs in US history—into a more robust retirement system that doubles the current payout to individuals would build upon the most stable components of the current system.

The president and Congress, in their budgetary duties, and the US Federal Reserve bank in its financial oversight capacity, have all the levers they need to ensure financial viability. This is a matter of politics, not economics. It is clear that the best way to stabilize and strengthen the retirement system, as well as the broader national economy itself, is to expand Social Security, bringing the American retirement system more in line with those in other developed societies. This can be accomplished by making the Social Security payroll tax fairer and more universally applied, by eliminating deductions for businesses that provide retirement plans (since that would be unnecessary with Social Security Plus), and by rolling back or limiting various tax-favored loopholes and deductions that massively favor wealthier Americans. Multiple mechanisms and plans are possible toward those goals.

More broadly, the United States must begin to view universal social insurance as a critical pillar of support for Americans and their families, as well as for US businesses that currently miss out on the competitive advantages that would come if retirement and health-care systems were not substantially employer based. The United States was once noted for its capacity for economic, political, and social innovation; in the aftermath of World War II, we created a land of broadly shared prosperity and opportunity, and starting in the 1960s began extending access to racial minorities, women, the LGBT community, and more. We have to rediscover our genius for that kind of innovation. We have to recognize that it *is* possible to create an affordable retirement system that is both decent *and* stable. This is not rocket science; it's a matter of political will, not a failure of design.

Retirement experts like Laurence Kotlikoff, Philip Moeller, and Paul Solman, in their best-selling "advice" book *Get What's Yours: The Secret to Maxing Out Your Social Security*, have provided a nice handbook on how to boost your Social Security benefit, using clever schemes like "file and suspend," "spousal benefits," and other brainy ploys.[23] But wouldn't it be better to have a retirement system that provides adequate income for seniors without having an accountant's insider knowledge of the byzantine rules and tricks? The enormous gap between what is needed and what is being proposed by the politicians and professionals is glaring evidence that we need a completely new and pragmatic approach.

As we have seen, we don't need to cut Social Security, or trim it, or pare it back, or privatize it, or raise the retirement age, or use chained CPI (consumer price index) to reduce the annual cost-of-living allowance. Even maintaining the status quo is woefully inadequate at this point. We need to *expand* Social Security, and we need to do it *now*. That is the only sensible solution to the retirement crisis. And we have a roadmap for how to get there:

TAX FAIRNESS = RETIREMENT SECURITY = ECONOMIC STABILITY

Any movement that seeks to enact expansion of Social Security must link that to a call for tax fairness, since that is the most salient source of the revenue needed to pay for the Plus system. By reallocating federal tax and expenditure priorities that currently provide huge financial advantages to a small number of better-off people and concentrating them instead on the vast majority of Americans, we can create a retirement system that will work for all of us, instead of some of us.

The creation of expanded Social Security Plus would provide a secure and comfortable retirement for every American, and contribute greatly toward a solid foundation from which to build a strong and vibrant twenty-first-century economy. Our retirees, our families, our businesses, and our communities deserve no less.

Acknowledgments

In writing this book, it struck me over and over how wise and visionary was the generation of leaders led by President Franklin Roosevelt. More than any other presidential administration before or since, Roosevelt's utilized the irreplaceable capacity of the "visible hand" of government to bring different sectors of Americans to the table and to create pools of social insurance that to this day still help protect most Americans against the unpredictable vagaries of life. Those of us living today are standing upon their mighty shoulders as we try to chart a course forward for the challenges of our era. I pray that we get it right.

If we do get it right, it will be greatly the result of many of the indefatigable Americans who have fought to maintain that legacy. Inside my own intellectual geodesic dome, my thoughts on this subject and more have been immeasurably enriched by some of my colleagues at the New America Foundation, including Sherle Schwenninger, Michael Lind, and Joshua Freedman. I coauthored a paper on expanding Social Security with Mike, Josh, and Robbie Hiltonsmith from Dēmos, which became an important foundation for this present book. Thanks to all of them for keeping our eyes on the prize.

I also would like to thank others who have provided a treasury of encouragement and insights, whether directly or indirectly, including Dean Baker and Nicole Woo of the Center for Economic Policy and Research, Peter Richardson, and Jacob Hacker, and also to longtime Social Security stalwarts Nancy Altman, Eric Kingson, Teresa Ghilarducci, Michael Hiltzik, Robert Reich, Elizabeth Warren, Adam Green, Stephanie Taylor, and the Progressive Change Campaign Committee, Robert Ball, Jeff Madrick,

Len Burman, and Jeffrey Rohaly from the Urban-Brookings Tax Policy Center, Max Skidmore, Paul Krugman, and others.

Thank you to my editor at Beacon Press, Joanna Green, for shepherding this project to the right pasture, and also to managing editor Susan Lumenello, production director Marcy Barnes, and associate publisher Tom Hallock, who helped to bring this project to fruition.

And thank you once again to my partner, Lucy Colvin, for her love, support, and encouragement. Thank you one and all.

Notes

Introduction

1. Franklin D. Roosevelt, "Second Inaugural Address," Washington, DC, January 20, 1937, http://www.bartleby.com/124/pres50.html.
2. Elizabeth Warren, "The Retirement Crisis," floor speech, US Senate, November 18, 2013.
3. Michael Lind, Steven Hill, Robert Hiltonsmith, and Joshua Freedman, "Expanded Social Security: A Plan to Increase Retirement Security for All Americans," New America Foundation, April 2013, p. 1, https://static.newamerica.org/attachments/4219-expanded-social-security /LindHillHiltonsmithFreedman_ExpandedSocialSecurity_04_03_13.5f 4f8f6f247843f58f496232b0cea69d.pdf.
4. Gaetano Mosca, *The Ruling Class* (orig. 1939; New York: Greenwood, 1980); James H. Meisel, *The Myth of the Ruling Class: Gaetano Mosca and the Elite* (Ann Arbor: University of Michigan Press, 1962), v.
5. Jill Braunstein, "Hard Choices on Social Security: Survey Finds Most Americans Would Pay More to Fix Its Finances and Improve Benefits," press release, National Academy of Social Insurance, October 23, 2014, https://www.nasi.org/press/releases/2014/10/press-release-hard-choices -social-security-survey-finds-m.
6. Ibid.
7. The Congressional Budget Office projects that Social Security can pay all scheduled benefits out of its own dedicated tax revenue stream (the current payroll tax, plus its investment income, which is banked into the Social Security Trust Fund) through at least 2033. After that, it will be able to pay 75 percent of benefits, assuming no other reforms are enacted.
8. Benjamin I. Page, Larry M. Bartels, and Jason Seawright, "Democracy and the Policy Preferences of Wealthy Americans," *Perspectives on Politics* 11, no. 1 (March 2013): 56–57, http://faculty.wcas.northwestern .edu/~jnd260/cab/CAB2012%20-%20Page1.pdf.
9. Social Security Administration, "Monthly Statistical Snapshot, August 2015," September 2015, table 2, http://www.ssa.gov/policy/docs/quick facts/stat_snapshot/#table2.

10. Oxford Martin School, "Oxford Martin School Study Shows Nearly Half of US Jobs Could Be at Risk of Computerisation," news release, September 18, 2013, http://www.futuretech.ox.ac.uk/news-release-oxford-martin-school-study-shows-nearly-half-us-jobs-could-be-risk-computerisation.

11. Andy Mukherjee, "Robots May Spell 'Control-Alt-Delete' for Workers," Reuters, October 23, 2014, http://blogs.reuters.com/breakingviews/2014/10/23/robots-may-spell-control-alt-delete-for-workers/.

Chapter One

1. Erin Carlyle, "9.7 Million Americans Still Have Underwater Homes, Zillow Says," *Forbes*, May 20, 2014, http://www.forbes.com/sites/erincarlyle/2014/05/20/9-7-million-americans-still-have-underwater-homes-zillow-says/.

2. Helaine Olen, "You Call This Retirement? Boomers Still Have Work to Do," *AARP The Magazine*, February/March 2014, http://www.aarp.org/work/retirement-planning/info-2014/boomer-retirement-little-savings-means-working.html; see also Teresa Ghilarducci, "Our Ridiculous Approach to Retirement," *New York Times*, July 21, 2012, http://www.nytimes.com/2012/07/22/opinion/sunday/our-ridiculous-approach-to-retirement.html.

3. Social Security Administration, "Understanding the Benefits," SSA Publication No. 05-10024, ICN 454930, June 2015, p. 4, http://www.ssa.gov/pubs/EN-05-10024.pdf.

4. Kathryn Anne Edwards, Anna Turner, and Alexander Hertel-Fernandez, *A Young Person's Guide to Social Security*, Economic Policy Institute, 2012, p. 6, http://www.nasi.org/sites/default/files/research/Young_Person%27s_Guide_to_Social_Security.pdf.

5. Bruce Bartlett, "GOP Cuts Budget with an Axe Instead of a Scalpel," *Fiscal Times*, February 11, 2011, http://www.thefiscaltimes.com/Columns/2011/02/11/GOP-Cuts-Budget-with-an-Axe-Instead-of-a-Scalpel.

6. Roosevelt, "Second Inaugural Address."

7. See "Policy Basics: Where Do Federal Tax Revenues Come From?," Center on Budget and Policy Priorities, March 11, 2015, www.cbpp.org/cms/?fa=view&id=3822; Joel Friedman, *The Decline of Corporate Income Tax Revenues*, Center on Budget and Policy Priorities, October 24, 2003, pp. 4–5, http://www.cbpp.org//sites/default/files/atoms/files/10-16-03tax.pdf.

8. Jesse Bricker et al., "Changes in U.S. Family Finances from 2010 to 2013: Evidence from the Survey of Consumer Finances," *Federal Reserve Bulletin* 100, no. 4 (September 2014), http://www.federalreserve.gov/pubs/bulletin/2014/pdf/scf14.pdf, cited in Matt Bruenig, *The Top 10% of White Families Own Almost Everything* (New York: Dēmos, Septem-

ber 5, 2014), http://www.demos.org/blog/9/5/14/top-10-white-families
-own-almost-everything.

 9. Drew DeSilver, "U.S. Income Inequality, on Rise for Decades, Is Now
    Highest Since 1928," Fact Tank: News in the Numbers, December 5,
    2013, http://www.pewresearch.org/fact-tank/2013/12/05/u-s-income
    -inequality-on-rise-for-decades-is-now-highest-since-1928/.

10. Emmanuel Saez and Gabriel Zucman, "Wealth Inequality in the
    United States Since 2013: Evidence from Capitalized Income Tax Data"
    (working paper 20625, NBER Working Paper Series, October 2014),
    http://www.gabriel-zucman.eu/files/SaezZucman2014.pdf.

11. Tim Fernholz, "The Bottom Ninety Percent of US Families Are No
    Wealthier Than in 1986," *Quartz*, October 18, 2014, http://qz.com/283059
    /ninety-percent-of-us-families-are-no-wealthier-than-they-were-in-1986.

12. Floyd Norris, "Corporate Profits Grow and Wages Slide," *New York
    Times*, April 4, 2014, http://www.nytimes.com/2014/04/05/business
    /economy/corporate-profits-grow-ever-larger-as-slice-of-economy
    -as-wages-slide.html.

13. Barbara Garson, "Freelance Nation: When Good Jobs Turn to Bad,"
    Salon, August 20, 2013, http://www.salon.com/2013/08/20/freelance
    _nation_when_good_jobs_turn_to_bad_partner.

14. US Census Bureau, *Income, Poverty and Health Insurance Coverage in
    the United States: 2013*, September 16, 2014, http://www.census.gov
    /newsroom/press-releases/2014/cb14-169.html.

15. Michael Grabell, "The Expendables: How the Temps Who Power Cor-
    porate Giants Are Getting Crushed," *ProPublica*, June 27, 2013, http://
    www.propublica.org/article/the-expendables-how-the-temps-who
    -power-corporate-giants-are-getting-crushe.

16. National Employment Law Project, "The Low-Wage Recovery: Indus-
    try Employment and Wages Four Years into the Recovery," April 2014,
    p. 2, http://www.nelp.org/content/uploads/2015/03/Low-Wage-Recovery
    -Industry-Employment-Wages-2014-Report.pdf.

17. Angela Johnson, "76% of Americans are Living Paycheck-to-Paycheck,"
    CNN Money, June 24, 2013, http://money.cnn.com/2013/06/24/pf
    /emergency-savings.

18. "Freelancers Union and Upwork Release New Study Revealing Insights
    into the Almost 54 Million People Freelancing in America," *Upwork*,
    October 1, 2015, https://www.upwork.com/press/2015/10/01/freelancers
    -union-and-upwork-release-new-study-revealing-insights-into-the
    -almost-54-million-people-freelancing-in-america.

19. MBO Partners, *2014 State of Independence in America Report* (Herndon,
    VA: MBO Partners, 2014), http://info.mbopartners.com/rs/mbo/images
    /2014-MBO_Partners_State_of_Independence_Report.pdf; see also
    Susan Adams, "More Than a Third of U.S. Workers Are Freelancers

Now, But Is That Good for Them?," *Forbes*, September 5, 2014, http://www.forbes.com/sites/susanadams/2014/09/05/more-than-a-third-of-u-s-workers-are-freelancers-now-but-is-that-good-for-them/.

20. Mike Berg, *Invisible to Remarkable: In Today's Job Market, You Need to Sell Yourself as "Talent," Not Just Someone Looking for Work* (Bloomington, IN: iUniverse, 2012), 13.

21. Center on Budget and Policy Priorities, "Policy Basics: Top Ten Facts about Social Security," August 13, 2015, fact #6, http://www.cbpp.org/research/social-security/policy-basics-top-ten-facts-about-social-security.

22. Ibid., facts #8 and 9.

23. Laurence Kotlikoff, Philip Moeller, and Paul Solman, *Get What's Yours: The Secret to Maxing Out Your Social Security* (New York: Simon and Schuster, 2015), 6 and 20 for life expectancies.

24. Ibid., 252.

25. Ibid., 251.

26. David Welna, "To Fix Social Security, Some Democrats Want to Lift Wage Cap," National Public Radio, December 5, 2013, http://www.npr.org/2013/12/05/249068448/to-fix-social-security-some-democrats-want-to-lift-wage-cap.

27. Social Security Trustees, "The 2014 Annual Report of the Board Of Trustees of the Federal Old-Age and Survivors Insurance and Federal Disability Insurance Trust Funds," July 28, 2014, table 4.A1, www.ssa.gov/oact/TR/2014/IV_A_SRest.html#506116; Nancy Altman and Eric Kingson, *Social Security Works! Why Social Security Isn't Going Broke and How Expanding It Will Help Us All* (New York: New Press, 2015), 97.

28. Diane Oakley and Kelly Kenneally, "Retirement Security 2015: Roadmap for Policy Makers," National Institute on Retirement Security, March 2015, pp. 5, 8–9, http://www.nirsonline.org/storage/nirs/documents/2015%20Opinion%20Research/final_opinion_research_2015.pdf.

29. Alicia Williams, "Social Security 80th Anniversary Survey Report," AARP Research, August 2015, http://www.aarp.org/research/topics/economics/info-2015/social-security-80th-anniversary-report.html.

30. "Congressional Pensions Update," FactCheck.org, January 5, 2015, http://www.factcheck.org/2015/01/congressional-pensions-update/.

Chapter Two

1. US Securities and Exchange Commission, "Money Market Funds," April 22, 2015, https://www.sec.gov/spotlight/money-market.shtml.

2. Employee Benefit Research Institute, "FAQs About Benefits—Retirement Issues," 2014, www.ebri.org/publications/benfaq/index.cfm?fa=retfaq.

3. Altman and Kingson, *Social Security Works!*, 63.

4. Stephen Losey, "FERS Retirement Fund Projects Surplus," *Federal Times*, April 23, 2012, http://www.federaltimes.com/article/20120423 /BENEFITS02/204230302/FERS-retirement-fund-projects-surplus.

5. Michael Greenstone and Adam Looney, "A Record Decline in Government Jobs: Implications for the Economy and America's Workforce," *The Hamilton Project* (blog), Brookings Institution, August 3, 2012, http://www.brookings.edu/blogs/jobs/posts/2012/08/03-jobs-green stone-looney.

6. Greg Mennis, "The State Pensions Funding Gap: Challenges Persist," Pew Charitable Trusts, table: "State Public Pensions," July 14, 2015, http://www.pewtrusts.org/en/research-and-analysis/issue-briefs /2015/07/the-state-pensions-funding-gap-challenges-persist.

7. Kevin Cook, "Public Pension Liabilities in California," Public Policy Institute of California, July 2015, http://www.ppic.org/main/publica tion_show.asp?i=1157.

8. Mary Williams Walsh, "Next School Crisis for Chicago: Pension Fund Is Running Dry," *New York Times*, September 19, 2012, http://www .nytimes.com/2012/09/20/business/teachers-pension-a-big-issue-for -chicago.html.

9. David Chen and Mary Williams Walsh, "New York City Pension System Is Strained by Costs and Politics," *New York Times*, August 3, 2014, http://www.nytimes.com/2014/08/04/nyregion/new-york-city-pension -system-is-strained-by-costs-and-politics.html.

10. Mike DeBonis, "D.C.'s Pensions Are Looking Pretty," *Washington Post*, March 11, 2013, https://www.washingtonpost.com/blogs/mike-debonis /wp/2013/03/11/d-c-s-pensions-are-looking-pretty.

11. Barbara A. Butrica, "Retirement Plan Assets," Urban Institute, Program on Retirement Policy, January 2013, http://www.urban.org /UploadedPDF/412622-Retirement-Plan-Assets.pdf.

12. Sarah Anderson and Scott Klinger, "A Pension Deficit Disorder: The Massive CEO Retirement Funds and Underfunded Worker Pensions at Firms Pushing Social Security Cuts," Institute for Policy Studies, November 27, 2012, http://www.ips-dc.org/pension-deficit-disorder.

13. Floyd Norris, "Private Pension Plans, Even at Big Companies, May Be Underfunded," *New York Times*, July 20, 2012, http://www.nytimes .com/2012/07/21/business/pension-plans-increasingly-underfunded-at -largest-companies.html.

14. Ibid.

15. Frances Denmark, "Can the Teamsters Save Union Pensions?," *Institutional Investor*, May 20, 2014, http://www.institutionalinvestor.com /article/3343595/investors-pensions/can-the-teamsters-save-union -pensions.html.

16. Patrick Purcell, "Income of Americans Aged 65 and Over, 1968–2008,"

Congressional Research Service, November 4, 2009, pp. 2–3, http://
digitalcommons.ilr.cornell.edu/key_workplace/675/.

17. Employee Benefit Research Institute, "FAQs About Benefits."
18. Employee Benefit Research Institute, "Trends in Defined Benefit Pension Plans," 2012, http://www.ebri.org/publications/benfaq/index
.cfm?fa=retfaqt14fig1. Data varies by source: see also the Center for
Retirement Research at Boston College (1989–2010 data: http://crr
.bc.edu/wp-content/uploads/1980/04/Pension-coverage.pdf) and the
Bureau of Labor Statistics (current data: http://www.bls.gov/ncs/ebs
/benefits/2012/ownership/private/table02a.htm).
19. Robert Hiltonsmith, *The Failure of the 401(k): How Individual Retirement Plans Are a Costly Gamble for American Workers* (New York:
Dēmos, November 9, 2010), http://www.demos.org/publication
/failure-401k-how-individual-retirement-plans-are-costly-gamble
-american-workers.
20. Alicia Munnell and Matthew Rutledge, "The Effects of the Great Recession on the Retirement Security of Older Workers" (working paper
#13–03, National Poverty Center: Working Paper Series, March 2013),
http://npc.umich.edu/publications/u/2013-03-npc-working-paper.pdf.
21. Brad M. Barber and Terrance Odean, "The Behavior of Individual Investors," SSRN eLibrary, September 7, 2011, http://papers.ssrn.com
/sol3/papers.cfm?abstract_id=1872211.
22. Chris Farrell, "The 401(k) Turns Thirty Years Old," *Bloomberg Business*,
March 15, 2010, http://www.bloomberg.com/bw/stories/2010-03-15
/the-401-k-turns-thirty-years-oldbusinessweek-business-news-stock
-market-and-financial-advice.
23. David Ignatius, "The Baby Boomers' Retirement Bummer," *Washington Post*, May 7, 2009, http://www.washingtonpost.com/wp-dyn/con
tent/article/2009/05/06/AR2009050603322.html.
24. Steven Hill, "Secure Retirement for All Americans," Policy paper, New
America Foundation, August 16, 2010, http://www.newamerica.org/eco
nomic-growth/secure-retirement-for-all-americans/; see also Alicia H.
Munnell, Anthony Webb, and Francesca N. Golub-Sass, "How Much
to Save for a Secure Retirement," Center for Retirement Research at
Boston College, November 2011, http://crr.bc.edu/briefs/how-much
-to-save-for-a-secure-retirement/.
25. Teresa Ghilarducci, "Our Ridiculous Approach to Retirement," *New
York Times*, July 21, 2012, http://www.nytimes.com/2012/07/22/opinion
/sunday/our-ridiculous-approach-to-retirement.html. See also Nari
Rhee, "The Retirement Savings Crisis: Is It Worse Than We Think?,"
National Institute on Retirement Security, June 2013, p. 12, "Figure 9:
Typical Working-Age Household Has Only $3,000 in Retirement Account Assets; Typical Near-Retirement Household Has Only $12,000,"

http://www.nirsonline.org/storage/nirs/documents/Retirement%20Sav
ings%20Crisis/retirementsavingscrisis_final.pdf; Olen, "You Call This
Retirement?"

26. Alicia H. Munnell, Anthony Webb, and Francesca Golub-Sass, "The
   National Retirement Risk Index: After the Crash," Center for Retirement Research at Boston College, October 2009, http://www.oecd.org
   /finance/private-pensions/46263009.pdf; Alicia H. Munnell, "Falling
   Short: The Coming Retirement Crisis and What to Do About It,"
   Center for Retirement Research at Boston College, April 2015, no. 15-7,
   p. 2, figure 2: "The National Retirement Risk Index, 1983–2013," http://
   crr.bc.edu/wp-content/uploads/2015/04/IB_15-7_508.pdf.
27. Kotlikoff, Moeller, and Solman, *Get What's Yours*, 13.
28. Yeva Nersisyan and L. Randall Wray, "The Trouble with Pensions:
   Toward an Alternative Public Policy to Support Retirement," public
   policy brief, Levy Economics Institute of Bard College, no. 109 (March
   2010): 3–4, 11–12.
29. Robert Hiltonsmith, *The Retirement Savings Drain: The Hidden and
   Excessive Costs of 401(k)s* (New York: Dēmos, May 29, 2012), http://
   www.demos.org/publication/retirement-savings-drain-hidden-exces
   sive-costs-401ks.
30. Income earners in the top quintile gained a benefit equal to 3.2 percent of their income, while individuals in the three middle quintiles,
   and who already make much less money, only gained a benefit equal
   to about 0.9 percent of their income. Josh Freedman, "The Tax Break
   Myth: They're Not Really for the Middle Class," *Atlantic*, November 1,
   2012, http://www.theatlantic.com/business/archive/2012/11/the-tax
   -break-myth-theyre-not-really-for-the-middle-class/264388/.
31. Tax Policy Center, "T12–0244—Distribution of Itemized Deductions
   by Cash Income Percentile, 2011," October 3, 2012, http://www.taxpolicy
   center.org/numbers/displayatab.cfm?Docid=3549.
32. Congressional Budget Office, *The Budget and Economic Outlook: 2014 to
   2024*, February 4, 2014, https://www.cbo.gov/publication/45010.
33. Kotlikoff, Moeller, and Solman, *Get What's Yours*, 256.
34. Federal Reserve Board of the United States, *Flow of Funds Accounts
   of the United States*, Z.1, March 11, 2010, table B.100: "Balance Sheet of
   Households and Nonprofit Organizations," www.federalreserve.gov
   /releases/z1/20100311/z1r-5.pdf.
35. Carlyle, "9.7 Million Americans Still Have Underwater Homes."
36. Alexander Reisenbichler, "Safe as Houses: Comparing Housing Finance
   Policies in the U.S. and Germany," American Institute for Contempo-
   rary German Studies (AICGS), September 26, 2014, http://www.aicgs
   .org/publication/safe-as-houses-comparing-housing-finance-policies
   -in-the-u-s-and-germany/.

37. Paul Krugman, "The Insecure American," *New York Times*, May 29, 2015, http://www.nytimes.com/2015/05/29/opinion/paul-krugman-the -insecure-american.html; Board of Governors of the Federal Reserve System, *Report on the Economic Well-Being of U.S. Households in 2014* (Washington, DC: Board of Governors of the Federal Reserve System, May 2015), 1–3, http://www.federalreserve.gov/econresdata/2014-report -economic-well-being-us-households-201505.pdf.

38. Jennifer Brooks and Kasey Wiedrich, "Assets and Opportunity Score-card 2013—Living on the Edge: Financial Insecurity and Policies to Rebuild Prosperity in America," Corporation for Enterprise Development, January 2013, http://assetsandopportunity.org/assets/pdf/2013 _Scorecard_Report.pdf.

39. Charles Delafuente, "Borrowing from the Future," *New York Times*, February 11, 2013, http://www.nytimes.com/2013/02/12/business/early -withdrawals-plague-retirement-accounts-study-says.html.

40. "Should Congress Limit the Mortgage-Interest Deduction?," *Wall Street Journal*, March 16, 2014, http://www.wsj.com/articles/SB10001424 052702304709904579407111906612936.

41. US Office of Management and Budget, *Federal Receipts*, 2014, http:// www.whitehouse.gov/sites/default/files/omb/budget/fy2015/assets /receipts.pdf.

42. Ibid.

43. Beadsie Woo, Ida Rademacher, and Jillien Meier, *Upside Down: The $400 Billion Federal Asset-Building Budget* (Baltimore: Corporation for Enterprise Development, 2010), http://cfed.org/assets/pdfs/Upside Down_final.pdf.

44. US Office of Management and Budget, "Table 4.1—Outlays by Agency: 1962–2019," http://www.whitehouse.gov/sites/default/files/omb/budget /fy2015/assets/hist04z1.xls (last accessed September 2014).

45. Will Fischer and Barbara Sard, "Chart Book: Federal Housing Spend-ing Is Poorly Matched to Need: Tilt Toward Well-Off Homeowners Leaves Struggling Low-Income Renters Without Help," Center on Budget and Policy Priorities, December 18, 2013, http://www.cbpp.org /cms/?fa=view&id=4067.

46. Teresa Ghilarducci, http://teresaghilarducci.org.

Chapter Three

1. Braunstein, "Hard Choices on Social Security."

2. Douglas J. Amy, "The Anti-Government Campaign," Governmentis good.com, 2007, http://www.governmentisgood.com/articles.php ?aid=9.

3. Paul Krugman, "Spearing the Beast," *New York Times*, February 8, 2005, http://www.nytimes.com/2005/02/08/opinion/spearing-the-beast.html.

4. Pedro Nicolaci Da Costa, "Tax Cuts Boost Jobs, Just Not When Targeted at Rich," *Wall Street Journal*, April 20, 2015, http://blogs.wsj.com/economics/2015/04/20/tax-cuts-boost-jobs-just-not-when-targeted-at-rich.

5. David Madland, "Unwavering Fealty to a Failed Theory," *US News & World Report*, August 6, 2015, http://www.usnews.com/opinion/economic-intelligence/2015/08/06/republican-2016-candidates-cling-to-failed-trickle-down-economics-theory.

6. Corbett Daly, "Rick Perry Says Social Security Is a 'Ponzi Scheme' and a 'Monstrous Lie,'" CBS News, August 29, 2011, http://www.cbsnews.com/news/rick-perry-says-social-security-is-a-ponzi-scheme-and-a-monstrous-lie.

7. Paul Krugman, "Pension-Cutters and Privatizers, Oh My," *New York Times*, August 19, 2015, http://krugman.blogs.nytimes.com/2015/08/19/pension-cutters-and-privatizers-oh-my.

8. Paul Krugman, "Republicans Against Retirement," *New York Times*, August 17, 2015, http://www.nytimes.com/2015/08/17/opinion/republicans-against-retirement.html.

9. Ezra Klein, "The Republican Party Doesn't Want to Believe Its Voters Agree with Trump. But They Do," *Vox*, August 17, 2015, http://www.vox.com/2015/8/17/9164241/donald-trump-issues.

10. John P. Avlon, "Republicans Wisely Break with Grover Norquist," CNN, November 28, 2012, http://www.cnn.com/2012/11/26/opinion/avlon-grover-norquist.

11. Michael Hiltzik, "Unmasking the Most Influential Billionaire in U.S. Politics," *Los Angeles Times*, October 2, 2012, http://articles.latimes.com/2012/oct/02/business/la-fi-hiltzik-20121003.

12. Alan Feuer, "Peter G. Peterson's Last Anti-Debt Crusade," *New York Times*, April 8, 2011, http://www.nytimes.com/2011/04/10/nyregion/10peterson.html.

13. Hiltzik, "Unmasking the Most Influential Billionaire."

14. *SourceWatch*, s.v. "Peter Peterson," March 8, 2015, http://www.sourcewatch.org/index.php/Peter_Peterson.

15. David Dayen, "America Speaks in LA—They Want Economic Recovery, No Social Security Cuts," *Shadowproof*, June 26, 2010, http://shadowproof.com/2010/06/26/america-speaks-in-la-they-want-economic-recovery-no-social-security-cuts/.

16. Thomas Frank, "Avoiding the Austerity Trap," *Wall Street Journal*, June 30, 2010, http://www.wsj.com/articles/SB10001424052748704103904575337223759366794.

17. Linda Douglas, "A Q&A with Barack Obama," *National Journal*, NBCNews.com, November 8, 2007, http://www.nbcnews.com/id/21693036/ns/politics-national_journal/t/qa-barack-obama.

18. Michael Shear, "Obama Pledges Reform of Social Security, Medicare Programs," *Washington Post,* January 16, 2009, http://www.washington post.com/wp-dyn/content/article/2009/01/15/AR2009011504114.html.
19. Emily Brandon, "How the Chained CPI Affects Social Security Payments," *US News & World Report,* April 29, 2013, http://money .usnews.com/money/retirement/articles/2013/04/29/how-the-chained-cpi-affects-social-security-payments.
20. "Transcript: Democratic Debate in Philadelphia," *New York Times,* April 16, 2008, http://www.nytimes.com/2008/04/16/us/politics/16text -debate.html.
21. Brooks Jackson, "Clinton vs. Obama," *Newsweek,* November 18, 2007, http://www.newsweek.com/clinton-vs-obama-96445.
22. Alex Seitz-Wald and Kailani Koenig, "Dems Have 'Strong Disagreement' on Social Security, Sanders Says," MSNBC, October 30, 2015, http://www.msnbc.com/msnbc/dems-have-strong-disagreement -social-security-sanders-says.
23. Nicole Woo, Cherrie Bucknor, and John Schmitt, "Who Would Pay More If the Social Security Payroll Tax Cap Were Raised or Scrapped?," Center for Economic Policy and Research, January 2015, http://www .cepr.net/publications/reports/who-would-pay-more-if-the-social -security-payroll-tax-cap-were-raised-or-scrapped.
24. Joan McCarter, "Did Hillary Clinton Just Take Social Security Cuts off the Table?," *Daily Kos,* April 20, 2015, http://www.dailykos.com /story/2015/04/20/1379050/-Did-Hillary-Clinton-just-take-Social -Security-cuts-off-the-nbsp-table.
25. Michael Tanner, "Clinton Wanted Social Security Privatized," Cato Institute, July 13, 2001, http://www.cato.org/publications/commentary /clinton-wanted-social-security-privatized.
26. Bradley Keoun, "Morgan Stanley at Brink of Collapse Got $107 Billion from Fed," *Bloomberg Business,* August 22, 2011, http://www.bloomberg .com/news/articles/2011-08-22/morgan-stanley-at-brink-of-collapse -got-107b-from-fed.
27. Kim Geiger, "Alan Simpson Pens Scathing Letter to 'Greedy Geezers' Retiree Group," *Los Angeles Times,* May 23, 2012, http://articles.latimes .com/2012/may/23/news/la-pn-alan-simpson-pens-scathing-letter-to -greedy-geezers-retiree-group-20120523; Stephanie Condon, "Alan Simpson: Social Security Is Like a 'Milk Cow with 310 Million Tits!'" CBS News, August 25, 2010, http://www.cbsnews.com/news/alan-simp son-social-security-is-like-a-milk-cow-with-310-million-tits.
28. Garry Wills, *Reagan's America: Innocents at Home* (New York: Doubleday, 1986), 329; Lou Cannon, *President Reagan: The Role of a Lifetime* (New York: Simon and Schuster, 1991), 243.
29. William Safire, "Third Rail," *New York Times,* February 18, 2007, http:// www.nytimes.com/2007/02/18/magazine/18wwlnsafire.t.html.

30. Ronald Reagan, "Letter to Congressional Leaders About the Social Security System—July 18, 1981," Social Security Administration, July 18, 1981, http://www.ssa.gov/history/reaganstmts.html#letter2.

31. Altman and Kingson, *Social Security Works!*, 148.

32. Social Security Administration, "Greenspan Commission: Report of the National Commission on Social Security Reform," January 1983, https://www.ssa.gov/history/reports/gspan.html.

33. Altman and Kingson, *Social Security Works!*, 150.

34. George W. Bush, "The 2001 President's Commission to Strengthen Social Security: President's Remarks at the Announcement of the Commission," Social Security Administration, May 2, 2001, https://www.ssa.gov/history/reports/pcsss/potus.html.

35. Altman and Kingson, *Social Security Works!*, 17.

36. Ibid., 147–48.

37. Executive Order no. 13531, *National Commission on Fiscal Responsibility and Reform*, February 18, 2001, https://www.whitehouse.gov/the-press-office/executive-order-national-commission-fiscal-responsibility-and-reform.

38. Mike Lofgren, "Confessions of a GOP Operative Who Left 'the Cult': 3 Things Everyone Must Know About the Lunatic-Filled Republican Party," *Truthout*, September 5, 2011, http://www.alternet.org/story/152305/confessions_of_a_gop_operative_who_left_"the_cult"%3A_3_things_everyone_must_know_about_the_lunatic-filled_republican_party.

39. Ibid.

40. Ibid.

41. David Catanese, "The Next Big Fight Between Hillary Clinton and Liberals," *New Republic*, November 7, 2013, http://www.newrepublic.com/article/115510/hillary-clintons-2016-campaign-liberals-press-her-entitlements.

42. Martin O'Malley, "Expanding Social Security So Americans Can Retire with Dignity," MartinO'Malley.com, August 2015, http://martinomalley.com/wp-content/uploads/2015/08/OMalley-Retirement-Security.pdf; Bernie Sanders, "Sanders Files Bill to Strengthen, Expand Social Security," Bernie Sanders: United States Senator for Vermont, March 12, 2015, http://www.sanders.senate.gov/newsroom/press-releases/sanders-calls-on-congress-to-strengthen-and-expand-social-security.

43. Steven Hill, *10 Steps to Repair American Democracy: A More Perfect Union; 2012 Election Edition* (Boulder, CO: Paradigm Press, 2012).

44. James Dao, "In Michigan, A Swing State, Bush Picks Words Carefully," *New York Times*, October 27, 2000, http://www.nytimes.com/2000/10/28/us/2000-campaign-texas-governor-michigan-swing-state-bush-picks-words-carefully.html.

45. Republicans in Congress had attempted their own version of triangulation in the months prior to the 2000 election. GOP legislative initiatives

were focused on introducing bills designed to blunt political attacks by adopting popular Democratic issues and reframing them in Republican terms. On one issue after another, including the minimum wage, gun control, managed care reform, and prescription drugs, GOP leaders aggressively sought to neutralize the Democrats' top legislative priorities before the November elections. But House Minority Leader Richard A. Gephardt (D-MO) accused Republicans of conducting a "David Copperfield Congress," in which they voiced their support for popular issues without visible action. "I think they are heavy into illusion," he said. See Juliet Eilperin, "Election Realities Spur Drug Benefit Plan from House GOP," *Washington Post*, April 26, 2000.

46. Lori Montgomery, "GOP Changes Tune on Cutting Social Security with Elections on the Line," *Washington Post*, October 23, 2014, http:// www.washingtonpost.com/business/economy/gop-changes-tune-on -cutting-social-security-with-elections-on-the-line/2014/10/23/d8e57 db2-5ad0-11e4-b812-38518ae74c67_story.html.

47. Ibid.

48. Lawrence R. Jacobs and Robert Y. Shapiro, *Politicians Don't Pander: Political Manipulation and the Loss of Democratic Responsiveness* (Chicago: University of Chicago Press, 2000); Steven Hill, "Divided We Stand: The Polarizing of American Politics," *National Civic Review*, Winter 2005, http://www.steven-hill.com/divided-we-stand -the-polarizing-of-american-politics/.

49. Donald Trump, *Time to Get Tough: Making America #1 Again* (New York: Regnery, 2011), 68–69.

50. Nancy Altman, "2015 Trustees Report Confirms That Expanding Social Security Is Fully Affordable," *Huffington Post*, July 22, 2015, http://www .huffingtonpost.com/nancy-altman/2015-trustees-report-conf_b_7850 206.html.

51. Mike Lofgren, *The Deep State: The Fall of the Constitution and the Rise of a Shadow Government* (New York: Viking, 2016).

Chapter Four

1. Ilan Moscovitz, "5 Huge Myths About Social Security," *The Motley Fool*, October 15, 2012, http://www.fool.com/retirement/general/2012/10/15/5 -huge-myths-about-social-security.aspx.

2. Altman, "2015 Trustees Report Confirms That Expanding Social Security Is Fully Affordable."

3. George W. Bush, "Transcript of State of the Union," CNN, February 3, 2005, http://www.cnn.com/2005/ALLPOLITICS/02/02/sotu.transcript.3.

4. Altman and Kingson, *Social Security Works!*, 168.

5. Gary Burtless, "Does Population Aging Represent a Crisis for Rich Societies?," Brookings Institution, January 2002, p. 3, http://www .brookings.edu/views/papers/burtless/20020106.pdf.

6. Gary Burtless, "Can Rich Countries Afford to Grow Old?," Brookings Institution, July 15, 2005, p. 13, http://www.brookings.edu/views/papers /burtless/20050715.pdf.

7. Krugman, "Insecure American"; Board of Governors of the Federal Reserve System, *Report on the Economic Well-Being of U.S. Households in 2014*, 1–3.

8. Peter G. Peterson, "The Salvation of Social Security," *New York Review of Books*, December 16, 1982, http://www.nybooks.com/articles/archives /1982/dec/16/the-salvation-of-social-security.

9. Alex Pareene, "New Group: America's Youth Cry Out for Sensible, Moderate Deficit Reduction," *Salon*, November 13, 2012, http://www .salon.com/2012/11/13/new_group_americas_youth_cry_out_for _sensible_moderate_deficit_reduction/.

10. Robert J. Samuelson, "We Need to Stop Coddling the Elderly," *Washington Post*, November 3, 2013, https://www.washingtonpost .com/opinions/robert-j-samuelson-we-need-to-stop-coddling-the -elderly/2013/11/03/4063ebc0-430f-11e3-a624-41d661b0bb78_story.html.

11. Robert J. Samuelson, "The True State of the Elderly," *Washington Post*, February 5, 2014, https://www.washingtonpost.com/opinions/robert -samuelson-the-true-state-of-the-elderly/2014/02/05/96cfb386-8e78 -11e3-b46a-5a3d0d2130da_story.html.

12. Altman and Kingson, *Social Security Works!*, 176.

13. Dean Baker, "The Kids Versus Seniors Line Doesn't Fit the Facts," Center for Economic and Policy Research, September 19, 2013, http://cepr .net/blogs/cepr-blog/the-kids-versus-seniors-line-doesnt-fit-the-facts.

14. Williams, "Social Security 80th Anniversary Survey Report."

15. Monique Morrissey, "Beyond 'Normal': Raising the Retirement Age Is the Wrong Approach for Social Security," Economic Policy Institute, January 26, 2011, http://www.epi.org/publication/bp287.

16. Monique Morrissey, "The Myth of Early Retirement Age," Economic Policy Institute, November 9, 2011, http://www.epi.org/publication /myth-early-retirement.

17. Altman and Kingson, *Social Security Works!*, 173.

18. Charles Ellis, Alicia Munnell, and Andrew Eschtruth, *Falling Short: The Coming Retirement Crisis and What to Do About It* (New York: Oxford University Press, 2015).

19. Alicia Munnell and Steven Sass, *Working Longer: The Solution to the Retirement Income Challenge* (Washington, DC: Brookings Institution Press, 2009).

20. Social Security and Medicare Boards of Trustees, "A Summary of the 2015 Annual Reports," Social Security Administration, July 22, 2015, http://www.ssa.gov/oact/trsum.

21. Associated Press, "With Social Security Disability Fund Going Broke by 2016, Congress Set for Partisan, Election-Year Showdown," Fox News,

August 9, 2015, http://www.foxnews.com/politics/2015/08/09/with
-social-security-disability-fund-going-broke-by-2016-congress-set-for.

22. Robert Pear, "Social Security Disability Benefits Face Cuts in 2016,
Trustees Say," *New York Times*, July 22, 2015, http://www.nytimes.com
/2015/07/23/us/disability-benefits-face-cuts-in-2016-trustees-say.html.

23. Larry Dewitt, "Details of Ida May Fuller's Payroll Tax Contributions,"
Social Security Administration Historian's Office, July 1996, https://ssa
.gov/history/idapayroll.html.

24. Steven Attewell, "Freedom from Fear: Using the Social Security Act to
Rebuild America's Social Safety Net," New America Foundation,
January 11, 2009, p. 4, http://www.academia.edu/4424824/Freedom
_From_Fear_-_Using_the_Social_Security_Act_to_Rebuild_America
_s_Social_Safety_Net.

25. Social Security Administration, "Social Security: A Brief History,"
SSA Publication No. 21-059, ICN 440000, May 2015, p. 21, https://
www.socialsecurity.gov/pubs/EN-21-059.pdf.

26. Social Security Administration, "Monthly Statistical Snapshot, July
2015," August 2015, table 2, http://www.ssa.gov/policy/docs/quickfacts
/stat_snapshot/index.html.

27. US Office of Management and Budget, *Mid-Session Review: Budget of
the U.S. Government, Fiscal Year 2009*, 2009, http://www.gpo.gov/fdsys
/pkg/BUDGET-2009-MSR/pdf/BUDGET-2009-MSR.pdf.

28. Attewell, "Freedom from Fear," 4–5.

29. Ibid., 5.

30. Organisation for Economic Co-operation and Development, "Compare
Your Country: Pensions at a Glance," "Adequate pensions" tab, https://
www.compareyourcountry.org/pensions?cr=oecd&cr1=oecd&lg=en&
page=1#, in *Pensions at a Glance 2013: OECD and G20 Indicators* (Paris:
OECD, 2013), doi: 10.1787/pension_glance-2013-en.

31. Organisation for Economic Co-operation and Development, "Compare
Your Country: Pensions at a Glance," "Social equity" tab, www.com
pareyourcountry.org/pensions?cr=oecd&cr1=oecd&lg=en&page=1#,
in *Pensions at a Glance 2013: OECD and G20 Indicators* (Paris: OECD,
2013), doi: 10.1787/pension_glance-2013-en.

32. David Snowden, "U.S. Ranks 19th in the World on 2015 Natixis Global
Retirement Security Index," press release, Natixis, February 10, 2015,
http://ngam.natixis.com/docs/282/659/GRI%202015%20US%20News
%20Release%20FINAL.pdf.

33. Ibid.

Chapter Five

1. Oxford Martin School, "Oxford Martin School Study Shows Nearly
Half of US Jobs Could Be at Risk of Computerisation."

2. Kotlikoff, Moeller, and Solman, *Get What's Yours*, 256.

3. Ibid.

4. Social Security Administration, "Understanding the Benefits," SSA Publication No. 05-10024, ICN 454930, June 2015, p. 4, http://www.ssa .gov/pubs/EN-05-10024.pdf.

5. That is assuming that Social Security benefits are maintained at current levels and that there are no additional cuts to the program. Because the predicted exhaustion of the Trust Fund will result in Social Security being able to pay out only 75 percent of scheduled benefits starting sometime in the 2030s, maintaining benefits will require policy changes to meet this shortfall. For the purposes of this proposal, I am assuming that this shortfall will be bridged. But if it is not, and benefits drop, this proposal for increasing revenue to Social Security would have to be adjusted.

6. Joseph Henchman, "Obama Would Lift Social Security Earnings Cap, but at a Lower Tax Rate," *The Tax Policy Blog*, Tax Foundation, July 8, 2008, http://taxfoundation.org/blog/obama-would-lift-social-security -earnings-cap-lower-tax-rate.

7. Woo, Bucknor, and Schmitt, "Who Would Pay More If the Social Security Payroll Tax Cap Were Raised or Scrapped?"

8. Office of the Actuary, "Letter to Representative Peter DeFazio," Social Security Administration, April 23, 2015, p. 22, table 1d: "Change in Long-Range Trust Fund Reserves / Unfunded Obligation," column 2: "Changes in OASDI Income," https://www.socialsecurity.gov/OACT /solvency/PDeFazio_20150423.pdf. The actuarial table shows an increase in revenue into the Trust Fund of around $160 billion per year for OASDI, which includes revenue for disability benefits (that's the DI part). But this analysis is only interested in the impact on retirement benefits, so that number is multiplied by 0.85, since Social Security revenue is split generally between retirement and disability on an 85–15 percent basis (with one slight complication: the Bipartisan Budget Act has shifted the split between retirement and disability for 2016–2018, so that the split will be more like 81–19 percent for those years).

9. As we saw in chapter 2, barely 15 percent of private-sector workers today have a guaranteed payout pension. But the percentage is much higher among public-sector employees, about 78 percent.

10. Congressional Budget Office, *The Distribution of Major Tax Expenditures in the Individual Income Tax System* (Washington, DC: Congressional Budget Office, May 2013), 16, https://www.cbo.gov/sites/default /files/113th-congress-2013-2014/reports/43768_DistributionTaxExpendi tures.pdf.

11. White House, *Fiscal Year 2016: Analytical Perspectives of the U.S. Government* (Washington, DC: US Government Printing Office, 2015), 240, table 14–3: "Income Tax Expenditures Ranked By Total Fiscal Year 2015–2024 Projected Revenue Effect," line item 145: "Defined benefit

employer plans," and 146: "Defined contribution employer plans," https://www.whitehouse.gov/sites/default/files/omb/budget/fy2016 /assets/spec.pdf.

12. Mark Zandi, "How to Cut the Deficit—and What Happens If We Don't," *Washington Post*, July 15, 2011, https://www.washingtonpost .com/opinions/moodys-economist-mark-zandi-how-to-cut-the-defi cit--and-the-trouble-if-we-dont/2011/07/14/gIQAKmX8FI_story.html.

13. Congressional Budget Office, *Distribution of Major Tax Expenditures*, 3, 6, 15, table 1: "Budgetary Effects of Selected Major Tax Expenditures, Fiscal Years 2013 to 2023," line item: "Preferential Tax Rates on Capital Gains and Dividends," and table 2: "Distribution of Selected Major Tax Expenditures, by Income Group, 2013," line item: "Preferential Tax Rates on Capital Gains and Dividends," https://www.cbo.gov/sites /default/files/113th-congress-2013-2014/reports/43768_DistributionTax Expenditures.pdf.

14. Robert B. Avery, Daniel Grodzicki, and Kevin B. Moore, "Estate vs. Capital Gains Taxation: An Evaluation of Prospective Policies for Tax-ing Wealth at the Time of Death" (working paper 28, Federal Reserve Board, 2013), 2, 18, http://www.federalreserve.gov/pubs/feds/2013 /201328/201328pap.pdf.

15. Lawrence H. Summers and Ed Balls, "Report of the Commission on Inclusive Prosperity," p. 125, appendix 1: "US Policy Response," https://cdn.americanprogress.org/wp-content/uploads/2015/01/IPC -PDF-U.S.appendix.pdf.

16. Bill Bischoff, "Capital Gains: At What Rate Will Your Long-Term Sales Be Taxed?," *MarketWatch*, February 23, 2015, http://www.marketwatch .com/story/capital-gains-at-what-rate-will-your-long-term-sales-be -taxed-2015–02–18; Robert Pear, "New Taxes to Take Effect to Fund Health Care Law," *New York Times*, December 8, 2012, http://www .nytimes.com/2012/12/09/us/politics/new-taxes-to-take-effect-to-fund -health-care-law.html.

17. White House, *Fiscal Year 2016: Analytical Perspectives of the U.S. Gov-ernment*, p. 240, table 14–3: "Income Tax Expenditures Ranked By Total Fiscal Year 2015–2024 Projected Revenue Effect," line item 72: "Step-Up Basis of Capital Gains at Death," https://www.whitehouse.gov/sites /default/files/omb/budget/fy2016/assets/spec.pdf.

18. Congressional Budget Office, *Distribution of Major Tax Expenditures*, 15, table 2, line item: "Capital gains on assets transferred at death," https://www.cbo.gov/sites/default/files/113th-congress-2013-2014/reports /43768_DistributionTaxExpenditures.pdf.

19. Here's how that calculation was made: the step-up in basis exemption resulted in a federal expenditure of $63 billion; so, assuming a 20 per-cent capital gains tax rate, that infers a total capital gains of $315 billion

that the step-up in basis rule was applied to. Applying the Social Security tax of 6.2 percent to the $315 billion yields $19.5 billion.

20. James Stewart, "Trump Lands a Blow Against Carried Interest Tax Loophole," *New York Times*, September 17, 2015, http://www.nytimes.com/2015/09/18/business/with-trump-as-foe-carried-interest-tax-loop hole-is-vulnerable.html.

21. Caroline Danielson, "The Food Stamp Program in California," Public Policy Institute of California, February 2014, http://www.ppic.org /main/publication_show.asp?i=870.

22. Stewart, "Trump Lands a Blow Against Carried Interest Tax Loophole."

23. Jeanne Sahadi, "Romney Paid 14% Effective Tax Rate in 2011," CNN Money, September 21, 2012, http://money.cnn.com/2012/09/21 /pf/taxes/romney-tax-return.

24. Stewart, "Trump Lands a Blow Against Carried Interest Tax Loophole."

25. Victor Fleischer, "How a Carried Interest Tax Could Raise $180 Billion," *New York Times*, June 5, 2015, http://www.nytimes.com/2015/06/06 /business/dealbook/how-a-carried-interest-tax-could-raise-180-billion .html.

26. "Face the Nation: Trump, Christie & Cruz," transcript, CBS News.com, August 23, 2015, http://www.cbsnews.com/news/face-the-nation-tran scripts-august-23-2015-trump-christie-cruz.

27. Stewart, "Trump Lands a Blow Against Carried Interest Tax Loophole."

28. Congressional Budget Office, *Distribution of Major Tax Expenditures*, 15, table 2, line item: "State and Local Taxes."

29. Reisenbichler, "Safe as Houses."

30. Alexandra Thornton and Harry Stein, "Who Wins and Who Loses? Debunking 7 Persistent Tax Reform Myths," Center for American Progress, October 22, 2015, https://www.americanprogress.org/issues /tax-reform/report/2015/10/22/123815/who-wins-and-who-loses/.

31. See Lind, Hill, Hiltonsmith, and Freedman, "Expanded Social Security."

32. Organisation for Economic Co-operation and Development, "Architecture of National Pension Systems," in *Pensions at a Glance 2011: Retirement-Income Systems in OECD and G20 Countries* (Paris: OECD, 2011), 107, doi: 10.1787/pension_glance-2011-10-en and http://www .oecd-ilibrary.org/docserver/download/8111011ec010.pdf?expires=14418 40670&id=id&accname=guest&checksum=E621B4751749A5CAC39C9F 8BE0ECF13C.

33. Robert Kuttner, "The Task Rabbit Economy," *American Prospect*, October 10, 2013, http://prospect.org/article/task-rabbit-economy.

34. Predecessors for converting Social Security into a "double-decker" system can be found in previous proposals, which have enjoyed the support of many experts all the way back to the 1930s. Purely public

two-tier or double-decker plans must not be confused with plans put forth by proponents of partial or total Social Security privatization who have sought to combine purely private, tax-favored defined-contribution plans with public flat minimal benefits for the poor.

35. Organisation for Economic Co-operation and Development, "Architecture of National Pension Systems," 107.

36. *Fiscal Year 2016*, 240, table 14–3.

37. Max Skidmore, *Securing America's Future* (Lanham, MD: Rowman and Littlefield, 2008), 96.

38. Stephen Fidler, "Flexible Payroll Tax May Be Finland's Greatest Export," *Wall Street Journal*, July 2, 2010.

39. Teresa Ghilarducci, Bridget Fisher, and Zachary Knauss, "Now Is the Time to Add Retirement Accounts to Social Security: The Guaranteed Retirement Account Proposal," Schwartz Center for Economic Policy Analysis and Department of Economics, New School for Social Research, Policy Note Series, June 2015, http://www.economicpolicy research.org/images/docs/retirement_security_background/GRA _3.0.pdf; Teresa Ghilarducci, "Guaranteed Retirement Accounts: Toward Retirement Income Security," EPI Briefing Paper # 204, November 20, 2007; Tom Harkin, "The Retirement Crisis and a Plan to Solve It," US Senate Committee on Health, Education, Labor, and Pensions (Washington, DC: July 2012).

40. Lind, Hill, Hiltonsmith, and Freedman, "Expanded Social Security," 16.

41. Juliette Cubanski, Giselle Casillas, and Anthony Damico, "Poverty Among Seniors: An Updated Analysis of National and State Level Poverty Rates Under the Official and Supplemental Poverty Measures," Kaiser Family Foundation, June 10, 2015, http://kff.org/medicare /issue-brief/poverty-among-seniors-an-updated-analysis-of-national -and-state-level-poverty-rates-under-the-official-and-supplemental -poverty-measures/.

Conclusion

1. Kerry A. Dolan, "Inside the 2014 Forbes 400: Facts and Figures About America's Wealthiest," *Forbes*, September 29, 2014, http://www.forbes .com/sites/kerryadolan/2014/09/29/inside-the-2014-forbes-400-facts -and-figures-about-americas-wealthiest/.

2. Amy B. Dean, "Workers Are Constantly on the Edge of the Knife," *Truthout*, September 12, 2014, www.truth-out.org/news/item/26120 -workers-are-constantly-on-the-edge-of-the-knife.

3. Clare O'Connor, "Report: Walmart Workers Cost Taxpayers $6.2 Billion in Public Assistance," *Forbes*, April 15, 2014, http://www .forbes.com/sites/clareoconnor/2014/04/15/report-walmart-workers -cost-taxpayers-6-2-billion-in-public-assistance/.

4. Kimiko, "Your #UberCHOPPER Is Arriving Now . . ." Uber, July 2, 2013, http://newsroom.uber.com/nyc/2013/07/uberchopper.

5. David Kirkpatrick, "Inside Sean Parker's Wedding: The Planning Details, the Menu, the Décor, and the Favors," *Vanity Fair*, September 2013, http://www.vanityfair.com/news/tech/2013/09/sean-parker-wedding-story.

6. Sam Biddle, "The Full Damage of Facebook Billionaire Sean Parker's Fantasy Wedding," *Valleywag* (blog), *Gawker*, June 4, 2013, http://valleywag.gawker.com/the-full-damage-of-facebook-billionaire-sean-parkers-f-511236497.

7. George Packer, "Change the World," *New Yorker*, May 27, 2013, http://www.newyorker.com/magazine/2013/05/27/change-the-world.

8. Rana Foroohar, "The Artful Dodgers: Companies That Flee the U.S. to Avoid Taxes Have Forgotten How They Got So Big in the First Place," *Time*, September 11, 2014, http://time.com/3326573/the-artful-dodgers/.

9. Norris, "Corporate Profits Grow and Wages Slide."

10. Friedman, *Decline of Corporate Income Tax Revenues*, 3.

11. See "Policy Basics"; Friedman, *Decline of Corporate Income Tax Revenues*, 4–5.

12. Robert Pear, "Health Care Gains, but Income Remains Stagnant, the White House Reports," *New York Times*, September 16, 2015, http://www.nytimes.com/2015/09/17/us/politics/census-bureau-poverty-rate-uninsured.html.

13. Bureau of Labor Statistics, "Alternative Measures of Labor Underutilization for States, Third Quarter of 2014 through Second Quarter of 2015 Averages," US Department of Labor, July 24, 2015, http://www.bls.gov/lau/stalt.htm.

14. Sherle R. Schwenninger, "U.S. and Europe: Shaping a New Model of Economic Development," New America Foundation, June 1, 2010, https://www.newamerica.org/economic-growth/us-and-europe-shaping-a-new-model-of-economic-development.

15. MBO Partners, *2014 State of Independence in America Report*; see also Adams, "More Than a Third of U.S. Workers Are Freelancers Now."

16. Steven Hill, *Raw Deal: How the "Uber Economy" and Runaway Capitalism Are Screwing American Workers* (New York: St. Martin's Press, 2015).

17. Mark McSherry, "Week Ahead: Let's Hope Churchill Was Wrong About Americans," *Forbes*, October 7, 2013, http://www.forbes.com/sites/markmcsherry/2013/10/07/week-ahead-lets-hope-churchill-was-wrong-about-americans.

18. Centers for Medicare and Medicaid Services, "Historical," CMS.gov, December 9, 2014, https://www.cms.gov/research-statistics-data-and

-systems/statistics-trends-and-reports/nationalhealthexpenddata/nationalhealthaccountshistorical.html.

19. "Health Expenditure, Total (% of GDP)," World Bank, 2010–2014, http://data.worldbank.org/indicator/SH.XPD.TOTL.ZS.

20. Steven Hill, *Europe's Promise: Why the European Way Is the Best Hope in an Insecure Age* (Berkeley: University of California Press, 2010), 77–92.

21. Ibid., 74.

22. Wouter Bos, "Europe's Social Democrats, Solidarity and Muslim Immigration," Globalist.com, December 9, 2005, http://theglobalist.com/StoryId.aspx?StoryId=4976.

23. Kotlikoff, Moeller, and Solman, *Get What's Yours.*

Bibliography

Alesina, Albert, and Edward L. Glaeser. *Fighting Poverty in the US and Europe: A World of Difference*. Oxford, UK: Oxford University Press, 2004.

Alperovitz, Gar. *What Then Must We Do? Straight Talk About the Next American Revolution*. White River Junction, VT: Chelsea Green Publishing, 2013.

Altman, Nancy. *The Battle for Social Security: From FDR's Vision to Bush's Gamble*. Hoboken, NJ: John Wiley and Sons, 2005.

Altman, Nancy, and Eric Kingson. *Social Security Works! Why Social Security Isn't Going Broke and How Expanding It Will Help Us All*. New York: New Press, 2015.

Baily, Martin Neil, and Jacob Funk Kirkegaard. *US Pension Reform: Lessons from Other Countries*. Washington, DC: Peterson Institute for International Economics, 2009.

Baker, Dean. "Debt, Deficits, and Demographics." New America Foundation, November 2012. http://nsc.newamerica.net/sites/newamerica.net/files /policydocs/Baker_Dean_DebtDeficitsDemographics_November2012.pdf.

Baker, Dean, and Mark Weisbrot. *Social Security: The Phony Crisis*. Chicago: University Of Chicago Press, 2000.

Barnes, Peter. *With Liberty and Dividends for All: How to Save Our Middle Class When Jobs Don't Pay Enough*. San Francisco: Berrett-Koehler Publishers, 2014.

Béland, Daniel. *Social Security: History and Politics from the New Deal to the Privatization Debate*. Lawrence: University Press of Kansas, 2005.

Berg, Mike. *Invisible to Remarkable: In Today's Job Market, You Need to Sell Yourself as "Talent," Not Just Someone Looking for Work*. Bloomington, IN: iUniverse, 2012.

Biggs, Andrew G. *Social Security: The Story of Its Past and a Vision for Its Future*. Washington, DC: AEI Press, 2011.

Bivens, Josh, Elise Gould, Lawrence Mishel, and Heidi Shierholz. *Raising America's Pay: Why It's Our Central Economic Policy Challenge*. Washington, DC: Economic Policy Institute, June 2014.

Board of Governors of the Federal Reserve System. *Report on the Economic Well-Being of US Households in 2014*. Washington, DC: Board

of Governors of the Federal Reserve System, May 2015. http://www
.federalreserve.gov/econresdata/2014-report-economic-well-being-us
-households-201505.pdf.

Butrica, Barbara A. "Retirement Plan Assets." Urban Institute, Program on
Retirement Policy, January 2013. http://www.urban.org/UploadedPDF
/412622-Retirement-Plan-Assets.pdf.

Cannon, Lou. *President Reagan: The Role of a Lifetime.* New York: Simon and
Schuster, 1991.

Clinton, Bill. *Back to Work: Why We Need Smart Government for a Strong
Economy.* New York: Knopf, 2011.

Conason, Joe. *The Raw Deal: How the Bush Republicans Plan to Destroy Social
Security and the Legacy of the New Deal.* Sausalito, CA: PoliPoint Press,
2005.

Congressional Budget Office. *The Distribution of Major Tax Expenditures in
the Individual Income Tax System.* Washington, DC: Congressional Budget Office, May 2013. https://www.cbo.gov/sites/default/files/113th-con
gress-2013-2014/reports/43768_DistributionTaxExpenditures.pdf.

Crain, Marion, and Michael Sherraden. *Working and Living in the Shadow of
Economic Fragility.* Oxford, UK: Oxford University Press, 2014.

Diamond, Peter, and Peter Orszag. *Saving Social Security: A Balanced Approach.* Washington, DC: Brookings Institution Press, 2003.

Ellis, Charles, Alicia Munnell, and Andrew Eschtruth. *Falling Short: The Coming Retirement Crisis and What to Do About It.* New York: Oxford University Press, 2015.

Federal Interagency Forum on Aging-Related Statistics. *Older Americans 2012:
Key Indicators of Well-Being.* Washington, DC: US Government Printing
Office, June 2012. http://www.agingstats.gov/Main_Site/Data/2012_Docu
ments/docs/EntireChartbook.pdf.

Frank, Robert, and Phillip Cook. *The Winner-Take-All Society: Why the Few at
the Top Get So Much More Than the Rest of Us.* New York: Free Press, 1995.

Friedman, Joel. *The Decline of Corporate Income Tax Revenues.* Center on
Budget and Policy Priorities, October 24, 2003. http://www.cbpp.org/sites
/default/files/atoms/files/10-16-03tax.pdf.

Garson, Barbara. *Down the Up Escalator: How the 99% Live in the Great Recession.* New York: Doubleday, 2013.

Ghilarducci, Teresa. "Guaranteed Retirement Accounts: Toward Retirement
Income Security," EPI Briefing Paper # 204, November 20, 2007.

———. *When I'm Sixty-Four: The Plot Against Pensions and the Plan to Save
Them.* Princeton, NJ: Princeton University Press, 2008.

Ghilarducci, Teresa, editor. *What You Need to Know About the Economics of
Growing Old* (*But Were Afraid to Ask): A Provocative Reference Guide to
the Economics of Aging.* Notre Dame, IN: Notre Dame Press, 2004.

Ghilarducci, Teresa, Bridget Fisher, and Zachary Knauss. *Now Is the Time to Add Retirement Accounts to Social Security: The Guaranteed Retirement Account Proposal.* Policy Note Series. New York: Schwartz Center for Economic Policy Analysis and Department of Economics, New School for Social Research, June 2015.

Gore, Al. *The Future: Six Drivers of Global Change.* New York: Random House, 2013.

Greenspan, Alan, and National Commission on Social Security Reform. *Report of the National Commission on Social Security Reform.* Chicago: Commerce Clearing House, January 1983. https://www.ssa.gov/history/reports/gspan.html.

Hacker, Jacob. *The Great Risk Shift: The Assault on American Jobs, Families, Health Care and Retirement and How You Can Fight Back.* New York: Oxford University Press, 2006.

Hacker, Jacob, and Paul Pierson. *Winner-Take-All Politics: How Washington Made the Rich Richer—and Turned Its Back on the Middle Class.* New York: Simon & Schuster, 2010.

Hill, Steven. "Divided We Stand: The Polarizing of American Politics." *National Civic Review,* Winter 2005. http://www.steven-hill.com/divided-we-stand-the-polarizing-of-american-politics/.

———. *Europe's Promise: Why the European Way Is the Best Hope in an Insecure Age.* Berkeley: University of California Press, 2010.

———. *Fixing Elections: The Failure of America's Winner Take All Politics.* New York: Routledge, 2002.

———. *Raw Deal: How the "Uber Economy" and Runaway Capitalism Are Screwing American Workers.* New York: St. Martin's Press, 2015.

———. "Secure Retirement for All Americans." Policy paper. New America Foundation, August 16, 2010. https://www.newamerica.org/economic-growth/secure-retirement-for-all-americans/.

———. *10 Steps to Repair American Democracy: A More Perfect Union; 2012 Election Edition.* Boulder, CO: Paradigm Publishers, 2012.

Hiltonsmith, Robert. *The Failure of the 401(k): How Individual Retirement Plans Are a Costly Gamble for American Workers.* New York: Dēmos, November 9, 2010. http://www.demos.org/publication/failure-401k-how-individual-retirement-plans-are-costly-gamble-american-workers.

———. *The Retirement Savings Drain: The Hidden and Excessive Costs of 401(k)s.* New York: Dēmos, May 29, 2012. http://www.demos.org/publication/retirement-savings-drain-hidden-excessive-costs-401ks.

Hiltzik, Michael. *The Plot Against Social Security: How the Bush Plan Is Endangering Our Financial Future.* New York: HarperCollins, 2005.

Hudson, Robert, editor. *The New Politics of Old Age Policy.* Baltimore: Johns Hopkins University Press, 2005.

Jacobs, Lawrence R., and Robert Y. Shapiro. *Politicians Don't Pander: Political Manipulation and the Loss of Democratic Responsiveness.* Chicago: University of Chicago Press, 2000.

Kaletsky, Anatole. *Capitalism 4.0: The Birth of a New Economy in the Aftermath of Crisis.* New York: PublicAffairs, 2010.

Kingson, Eric, and Edward D. Berkowitz. *Social Security and Medicare: A Policy Primer.* Westport, CT: Praeger, 1993.

Kornbluth, Jacob. *Inequality for All.* Documentary film. Los Angeles: 72 Productions. September 27, 2013. http://inequalityforall.com/.

Kotlikoff, Laurence, Philip Moeller, and Paul Solman. *Get What's Yours: The Secret to Maxing Out Your Social Security.* New York: Simon and Schuster, 2015.

Landes, David. *The Wealth and Poverty of Nations: Why Some Are So Rich and Some So Poor.* New York: W. W. Norton, 1999.

Laursen, Eric. *The People's Pension: The Struggle to Defend Social Security Since Reagan.* Oakland: AK Press, 2012.

Lind, Michael. *Land of Promise: An Economic History of the United States.* New York: Harper, 2013.

Lind, Michael, Steven Hill, Robert Hiltonsmith, and Joshua Freedman. "Expanded Social Security: A Plan to Increase Retirement Security for All Americans." Washington, DC: New America Foundation, April 2013. https://static.newamerica.org/attachments/4219-expanded-social-security /LindHillHiltonsmithFreedman_ExpandedSocialSecurity_04_03_13.5f4f8 f6f247843f58f496232b0cea69d.pdf.

Lofgren, Mike. *The Deep State: The Fall of the Constitution and the Rise of a Shadow Government.* New York: Viking, 2016.

———. *The Party Is Over: How Republicans Went Crazy, Democrats Became Useless, and the Middle Class Got Shafted.* New York: Penguin, 2012.

Madrick, Jeff. *The Case for Big Government.* Princeton, NJ: Princeton University Press, 2009.

———. *Seven Bad Ideas: How Mainstream Economists Have Damaged America and the World.* New York: Knopf, 2014.

Meisel, James H. *The Myth of the Ruling Class: Gaetano Mosca and the Elite.* Ann Arbor: University of Michigan Press, 1962.

Mosca, Gaetano. *The Ruling Class.* New York: Greenwood, 1980. First published 1939 by McGraw-Hill.

Munnell, Alicia, and Matthew Rutledge. "The Effects of the Great Recession on the Retirement Security of Older Workers." National Poverty Center, Working Paper Series: Working Paper #13–03, March 2013. http://npc .umich.edu/publications/u/2013-03-npc-working-paper.pdf.

Munnell, Alicia, and Steven Sass. *Working Longer: The Solution to the Retirement Income Challenge.* Washington, DC: Brookings Institution Press, 2009.

Munnell, Alicia H., Anthony Webb, and Francesca Golub-Sass. *The National Retirement Risk Index: An Update*. No. 12-20. Chestnut Hill, MA: Center for Retirement Research, Boston College, October 2012. http://crr.bc.edu /briefs/the-national-retirement-risk-index-an-update/.

Noah, Timothy. *The Great Divergence: America's Growing Inequality Crisis and What We Can Do About It*. New York: Bloomsbury Press, 2012.

Organization of Economic Cooperation and Development. "Architecture of National Pension Systems." In *Pensions at a Glance 2011: Retirement-Income Systems in OECD and G20 Countries*. Paris: OECD Publishing, 2011. http://dx.doi.org/10.1787/pension_glance-2011-10-en.

Page, Benjamin I., Larry M. Bartels, and Jason Seawright. "Democracy and the Policy Preferences of Wealthy Americans." *Perspectives on Politics* 11, no. 1 (March 2013), http://faculty.wcas.northwestern.edu/~jnd260/cab /CAB2012%20-%20Page1.pdf.

Piketty, Thomas. *Capital in the Twenty-First Century*. Cambridge, MA: Harvard University Press, 2014.

Pontusson, Jonas. *Inequality and Prosperity: Social Europe vs. Liberal America*. Ithaca, NY: Cornell University Press, 2005.

Poo, Ai-Jen. *The Age of Dignity: Preparing for the Elder Boom in a Changing America*. New York: New Press, February 2015.

Reich, Robert. *Saving Capitalism: For the Many, Not the Few*. New York: Knopf, 2015.

Russell, James W. *Social Insecurity: 401(k)s and the Retirement Crisis*. Boston: Beacon Press, 2014.

Saez, Emmanuel, and Gabriel Zucman. "Wealth Inequality in the United States Since 2013: Evidence from Capitalized Income Tax Data." National Bureau of Economic Research, Working Paper Series: Working Paper 20625, October 2014. http://gabriel-zucman.eu/files/SaezZucman2014.pdf.

Schwenninger, Sherle, and Joshua Freedman. "America's Debt Problem: How Private Debt Is Holding Back Growth and Hurting the Middle Class." New America Foundation, June 16, 2014. http://newamerica.net/publica tions/policy/americas_debt_problem_0.

Schwenninger, Sherle, and Samuel Sherraden. "The US Economy After The Great Recession: America's Deleveraging and Recovery Experience." New America Foundation, March 4, 2014. http://newamerica.net/publications /policy/the_us_economy_after_the_great_recession.

Skidmore, Max. *In a Nation as Rich as Ours: Why Social Security Works and Why Its Enemies Are Wrong*. Boulder, CO: Westview Press, 1999.

Social Security Administration, Office of Retirement and Disability Policy. *Income of the Population 55 or Older, 2010*. Washington, DC: Social Security Administration, 2012. https://www.socialsecurity.gov/policy/docs /statcomps/income_pop55/2010/.

Steuerle, C. Eugene, and Jon M. Bakija. *Retooling Social Security for the 21st*

Century: Right and Wrong Approaches to Reform. Washington, DC: Urban Institute Press, 1994.

Stiglitz, Joseph. *The Price of Inequality: How Today's Divided Society Endangers Our Future.* New York: W. W. Norton, 2012.

Stiglitz, Joseph E., Amartya Sen, and Jean-Paul Fitoussi. *Mismeasuring Our Lives: Why GDP Doesn't Add Up: The Report by the Commission on the Measurement of Economic Performance and Social Progress.* New York: New Press, 2010.

Summers, Lawrence H., and Ed Balls, *Report of the Commission on Inclusive Prosperity.* Appendix 1: US Policy Response. Washington, DC: Center for American Progress, 2015. https://cdn.americanprogress.org/wp-content /uploads/2015/01/IPC-PDF-U.S.appendix.pdf.

Trump, Donald. *Time to Get Tough: Making America #1 Again.* New York: Regnery, 2011.

Tucker, Jasmine V., Virginia P. Reno, and Thomas N. Bethel. *Strengthening Social Security: What Do Americans Want?* Washington, DC: National Academy of Social Insurance, January 2013. http://www.nasi.org/sites /default/files/research/What_Do_Americans_Want.pdf.

US Congress. *The 2014 Annual Report of the Board of Trustees of the Federal Old-Age and Survivors Insurance and Federal Disability Insurance Trust Funds.* Washington, DC: US Government Printing Office, 2014.

———. *The 2015 Annual Report of the Board of Trustees of the Federal Old-Age and Survivors Insurance and Federal Disability Insurance Trust Funds.* Washington, DC: US Government Printing Office, 2015.

White House. *Fiscal Year 2016: Analytical Perspectives of the US Government.* Washington, DC: US Government Printing Office, 2015. https://www .whitehouse.gov/sites/default/files/omb/budget/fy2016/assets/spec.pdf.

Wilkinson, Richard, and Kate Pickett. *The Spirit Level: Why Greater Equality Makes Societies Stronger.* New York: Bloomsbury Press, 2009.

Wills, Garry. *Reagan's America: Innocents at Home.* New York: Doubleday, 1986.

Websites of Organizations That Specialize in Social Security

Bipartisan Policy Commission on Retirement Security and Personal Savings, http://bipartisanpolicy.org/commission-on-retirement-security-and -personal-savings/

Center for Economic and Policy Research, http://www.cepr.net

Center for Retirement Research at Boston College, http://crr.bc.edu

Commission to Modernize Social Security, http://modernizesocialsecurity.org

Economic Opportunity Institute, http://www.eoionline.org

Institute for Women's Policy Research, http://www.iwpr.org

Latinos for a Secure Retirement, http://latinosforasecureretirement.org

National Academy of Social Insurance, https://www.nasi.org

National Committee to Preserve Social Security and Medicare, http://www
.ncpssm.org

National Institute on Retirement Security, http://www.nirsonline.org

National Senior Citizens Law Center, http://nsclcarchives.org

Older Women's Economic Security Task Force (OWES) of the National
Council of Women's Organizations, http://www.ncwo-online.org

Retirement Equity Lab, http://www.economicpolicyresearch.org/index.php
/retirement-equity-lab

Schwartz Center for Economic Policy Analysis, http://www.economicpolicy
research.org

Social Security Works, http://www.socialsecurityworks.org

Index